Mariuca and Marilyn
Saying Goodbye to Mama's Club

Exploring the Effects of Undue Influence

Mariuca and Marilyn
Saying Goodbye to Mama's Club

Exploring the Effects of Undue Influence

Richard E. Kelly

Parker Ridge Publishing   Tucson, Arizona

Readers may contact the publisher at:
mariucaandmarilyn@gmail.com

This edition was prepared for publishing by
Ghost River Images
5350 East Fourth Street
Tucson, Arizona 85711
www.ghostriverimages.com

Cover and some interior art by Carl Wilson
www.carlwilsonart.com

Some B&W interior illustrations by Dan Sharp
www.dansharpart.com

ISBN 978-0-9795094-6-9

Library of Congress Control Number: 2015943117

Printed in the United States of America
June 2015

Contents

Preface 7

A Special Tribute to Marilyn 9

Dedication 11

Mariuca's Story: *It's Never Too Late* 13

Part One 13
    A Life-Changing Knock at the Door 14
    Childhood as a "True Believer" 16
    A New Life at Bethel 18
    Life at Bethel 20
    Shattered Dreams—Heartbreak and Heartache 21
    "Fair and Balanced"—Facing a Judicial Committee 23
    The "Joy of Sex"—or Lack Thereof 25
    Return to Bethel 27

Part Two 29
    A New Love 31
    A Heartbreaking Discovery 32
    A Judicial Split Decision 34
    A Complete Physical Breakdown 35
    Carl Shares His Account of Events 36

Part Three 41
    A Chance Event 41
    Living Two Lives 42
    A Sudden Change in Carl 43
    Seeking a Different Direction 44
    Recognizing the Realities of Undue Influence 46
    Unhappy at Home 48
    Carl and Mariuca Share Their "Secrets" 49
    Carefully Looking for a Change 52
    Gifts 52
    An Uncomfortable Romance 54
    The Elders Want Answers 57
    Sorting Things Out 58
    A Word from the Author 60
    Carl Speaks Up 60
    Mariuca gets the Last Word 63

An Afterthought: 64

Transitioning from Mariuca to Marilyn 67

Marilyn's Story—Set Up for Failure 69

Part One 69
    Being "Second-Class" 71
    Living Without Friends 73

An Unusual, Repressed Environment 74
A Change of Lifestyle 75
Part Two 77
A Surprise Phone Call 78
"The Man of Her Dreams" 79
This Time "the Real Deal" 80
Reconciliation and a Reunion 81
Marilyn Decides to Ask for Help 82
Part Three 85
A "Loving Arrangement" 86
My Parents Take a Stand 87
Our Trip to Nebraska 88
Part Four 91
An Afterthought 96
Marilyn Merges with Mariuca and Carl's Story 99
Undue Influence 105
What Is Undue Influence? 105
How and Why Do People Allow Themselves to
be Unduly Influenced? 106
What Kinds of Groups and People Use Undue Influence? 107
How Great of a Threat is Undue Influence to a Free Society? 108
Additional costs to society from groups that unduly
influence its members 109
How Can We Stop This Rapidly Expanding Menace
to a Free Society? 109
The big picture 109
At a personal level 110
Special needs 111
The need for therapy 111
Available resources 112
Best Practices & Resources 112
The Need for Research Projects 114
Are You Being Unduly Influenced? 115
A questionnaire 116
Where Do We Go from Here? 116
A Word from the Artist Who Designed the Book Cover 117
Acknowledgements 119

Preface

Since the murder of my sister, Marilyn, over seventeen years ago, I have tried to honor her life by writing two books about our unique, apocalyptic journeys while trapped in the high-control, fear-based world of Jehovah's Witnesses *(JWs)*.

This is a religious organization guided by old, self-absorbed men who obsessively worry about the next world, "quote mine the Bible" to prove they are appointed by God and, for some reason, are not held accountable for their harmful policies or false prophecies.

In this third book, my goal is to honor my sister's life by telling Mariuca's story, who like Marilyn, while growing up as a JW (Mama's Club), was taught by these so-called prophets that in God's eyes, females must be subjected to men.

Limiting the role of females is one of the many harmful beliefs of the Watchtower Society (the legal policy-maker for JWs), which is particularly toxic to the mind of girls, with negative long-term consequences when they become adults.

By sharing Mariuca's story, who as a girl was handicapped by Watchtower's policies, my goal is to shine a bright light on an aberrant Christian group that goes under the radar for liability of its misdeeds and lies, and *to inspire women* at any age to act in ways that demonstrate there is life after Watchtower if they leave.

Yes, Mariuca's story has a happy ending, unlike Marilyn's.

7

Mariuca is a survivor, a strong, courageous woman, who finds a way to undo massive amounts of misinformation, identify the phobias and fears induced by Watchtower, and discover her own truth. Not an easy task, as she was taught as a child to believe she was *in the truth*; that pleasing God, defined by Watchtower's leaders, was what life was all about, her ultimate truth. If she made God happy, per Watchtower's *undue influence**, He would reward her with everlasting life.

As you read and snuggle into the heart, hopes and mind of this modern-day heroine, you will cheer her on as she learns to navigate a world she was taught to fear as a girl, now looking for real truth and discovering her unique meaning for life; something denied her as a child.

I strongly believe that you will come to adore and embrace this remarkable lady, and the special man who helps open her eyes and the door of opportunity.

---

* *Undue Influence* is mental, moral or physical domination, which deprives an individual of independent judgment and substitutes another person's objectives in place of the individual's own. It is often characterized by excessive insistence, superiority of physical power, mind, or will, or pressure applied due to authority, position, or in relation to the strength of the person or group submitting to it.

A Special Tribute to Marilyn

I will also retell Marilyn's story, a final tribute to my sister, at the end of this book. It is my way of connecting her life story to a series of books—Mama's Club books—that would *not* have been written without the abrupt ending of her life and our mama's refusal to honor Marilyn's life after she died. In so doing, it is my way of thanking Marilyn for inspiring me to learn to write. And yes, Marilyn, you have made a difference for thousands—my goal is millions in the near future—of people. You did not die in vain.

Dedication

I want to dedicate this book to those women who I know that have broken free from the *undue influence* of the Watchtower Bible & Tract Society. All of these women are no longer tethered to the damaging policies and beliefs of this high-control religion—Jehovah's Witnesses. My sister, Marilyn, would have been very proud of every one of them. I know that I am.

So I am sending my love and appreciation to you Mickey "Danmera" Hudson, Renee Azar Seisler, Sue Booth, Dijana Evans, my wife, Helen Kelly, Stephanie Gardener, my daughter, Kimberly Waalkes, Barbara Anderson, Melissa Griebel, Amneris Cruz, Jennifer Treece, Joanna Foreman, Julia Douglas, Sue Hall, Sheridan Ward, Lydia Ruth Turner, Elizabeth Sorbo, Daintre Warn, Annette Getzschman, Mary Lou Steel, Marvina Fay Benzekri, Merice Ewart-Marshall, Nicole Yvonne, Teddy Marie McCarty, Courtney Waldon, Gayle Minette McCurdy, Denise Elder, Deyanira Gonzalez, Rachel Crowder, Maria Albert, Stephanie Hammond, Kerri Desmarais, Anna Macaluso, Valarie O'Connor, Tami Dickerson, Sharon Gondek Bushouse, Chantal Rancourt, Haupi Justice, Louise Goode, Eliza Bell, Raven Maureen Pence, Isabella Botticelli, Miju Kim Gracey, Brenda Lee, Mary Strauser, Jada Buchanan, Noel Blackwell Ross, Suzi Drums, Wendy Espley, Anni Schulz, Patricia Russell, Belinda Van Doorselaer, Bonnie Rosa, Kirsty Wilcox, Terri O'Sullivan, Melissa Parton, Karen

Morgan, Raychel Walker, Kirsten Easton, Cynthia Velasco Hampton, Jennica Meulenberg, Abby Rhodes, Claire Hendy, Towanda Curie, Deborah D'Agostin, Karen Snizek, Janel Marie, Pamela Wright Dickson, Stacy Youst Sillen, Kerry Louderback-Wood, Barbara Kohout, Libby Partridge, Jill Chandler, Melanie Murray, Babs Mason, Leticia Casanova, Julie Leon, Nicole Lunt, Leticia Becerra, Mary Aquilar Buttafuoco, Anne Marie DeSoto, Shelley Brammer Truesdell, Heidi Nordberg, Sharon Ortiz, Gina Melton, Debby Moody Shard, Debbie Dykstra, Norine Kasten, Jennifer Lee-Gutowski, Holly Jean Veldhuis, Noel Parsons, Mindy Veldhuis Mench, Catherine Walters, Debbie Kotte, Diane Metzler, Toni Kuilan, Kim Brooks, Alexus Daring, Gina Harrison, Aprylle Marie, Tritia Esquivel, Priskilla Vermeersch, Oriana Haeck, Delina Haeck, Sara Zeeb, Candace Conti, Frances Peters and Victoria Deverson.

I also want to give special tribute to the special women, whose inspiring stories will grace my fourth book, *Looking for the Truth—It's Not at Mama's Club*. They are Jeni Lundblom Valdez, Miranda Hammons, Cora Latham, Heidi Slettemo and Lee Marsh, my sister, fellow warrior, and President for Advocates for Awareness of Watchtower Abuses—AAWA at aawa.co.

Mariuca's Story: *It's Never Too Late*

Part One

It was an unusual response—something I don't normally do—triggered by an exceptionally well-written email from a *Growing Up in Mama's Club* reader, Mariuca Rofick. The reader was an ex-Jehovah's Witness (JW), who confessed of having labored ten years while living at Bethel, the world headquarters for JWs, which was then located in Brooklyn, New York.

I am not certain why, but I sensed Mariuca wanted to tell me more; that she was fishing for a non-judgmental listening ear. I was someone who had been there, done that. So at the end of a short email response, I asked her to tell me her life story; a request that I had never made to anyone based on a single email.

In less than twenty-four hours, Mariuca responded with a heart-wrenching reply. At the end of her long email, she wrote, "Sorry! I guess you didn't ask for my entire life story. Once I got going, I couldn't stop. I am heading to the car right now, but I will continue later this evening."

When she made good on her promise, I knew immediately that Mariuca's story begged to be told to a much larger audience of non-JWs, if she'd allow me to tell it; a story with egregious twists and turns, a dicey moral dilemma and a heart-warming love story for the ages, convincing readers that *it's never too late*.

A Life-Changing Knock at the Door

Mariuca was born in Detroit, Michigan on March 7, 1965, two months before my son, Keith, was born. Her mom claims Mariuca entered this world a lady, a regal child, a quick learner with an even temperament. She took control seamlessly whenever necessary, although she could be bossy at times, according to her three siblings.

However, when she was five years old, something very strange happened, which dramatically changed her life.

Mariuca's mother was busy working her magic in the kitchen when she heard a loud series of persistent knocks at the front door. Pork chops were browning in the frying pan and potatoes were near their boiling point, but she decided to stop for a moment to see who was knocking.

When she opened the door, a well-dressed woman greeted her with a contagious smile and an interesting proposal. "My name is Deanna Smoot and I have some especially good news to share with you. Would it be okay to come inside for fifteen minutes to tell my story?"

Mariuca's mom said she was preparing dinner and now was not a good time. If Mrs. Smoot would jot down her telephone number, she would call her in the next few weeks. A long-time JW, Mrs. Smoot had never heard that excuse before. But three weeks later, she received the promised call from Mariuca's mother.

To make a long story short, a JW-style "Bible study" was started. A year later Mariuca's family joined Mama's Club—Jehovah's Witnesses. But *why* people become Witnesses *is* an important part of this story. However, one first needs to know that JWs think *how* one becomes a member is far more important than *why*.

Jehovah's Witnesses love to share interesting and unlikely stories about how this happens. My mother loved to hear those kinds of stories because they reinforced her belief that JWs were the only group that had "the truth" about God Almighty and actually *knew how* to make God happy.

14

It was even better if someone told a story at a large JW convention about a family he or she converted; it was like the bragging rush one gets at multi-level marketing events when reporting personal sales and recruiting successes. And my mama was invited to take center stage many times, always loving the opportunity.

Somehow, conversion stories at conventions were the ultimate confirmation that Jehovah God works in strange and wonderful ways to bring people into the truth.

And so it was with Deanna Smoot. She became an instant hero with her circuit assembly story about how the Rofick family became JWs.

"It was cold when I knocked on her door," Deanna said. "I wanted to come inside. When the lady said she was too busy to talk, but wanted my phone number and would call me, I was speechless. I had never heard that excuse before. I gave her my number, knowing it was a waste of time.

"So when I actually received a call from Mrs. Rofick, it took me by surprise. I told her that I hadn't expected her to call.

"She, in turn, seemed miffed by my reaction, saying, 'I told you I'd call, didn't I?' Mrs. Rofick didn't have a clue what the fuss was about. That would change when she became a JW and learned what the astronomical odds are of a householder calling you back."

This story received a loud ovation from those attending the assembly. But I wonder how the audience would have reacted had I, Richard Kelly, told the story this way:

"Mrs. Rofick joined because she wasn't happy with her life. She had periods of depression and often lost her temper, even in front of Mariuca and her younger brother. She married young, with little training on how to raise a family. She had serious questions about God, the purpose of life, and life after death—questions she could not answer. Deanna Smoot claimed she had the answers.

"Deanna was also very likable, had an air of confidence, and she knew her Bible. Oh, how she knew her Bible! At least that's what Mrs. Rofick thought. She didn't have a clue how well-trained Deanna was in 'cherry picking' verses to make it look like she actually was a Bible scholar."

I also would have told everyone at the assembly, "When Mariuca's dad found out his wife was studying with JWs, he was not happy. He was convinced that JWs were false religion in capital letters, a cult. Let someone visit with him if they dared and he'd make quick work of their nonsense.

"He was in good fighting form when an articulate, charismatic married couple met every one of his poorly thought-out theological punches. Mariuca's dad was impressed with the messengers and decided their message must be legitimate.

"He was looking for a community that would embrace him for his cultural diversity. His father was Bangladeshi and his mother African-American. While he didn't lack for self-esteem, he wanted to feel needed and valued for his uniqueness.

"He took an instant liking to the well-dressed couple who told him that God had a plan and an organization of hard-working followers that could use a man of his caliber. They answered all his questions, unaware that they were programmed to give him the impression that they really understood the Bible."

I am certain I would have been booed off the stage with a speech like that. But the reader needs to be aware of a grievous handicap which JWs exploit very well.

Mariuca's parents seldom read the Bible, and yet they passionately believed it was "the sacred word of God." They had no idea of what reputable scholars had been saying about the Bible for over two hundred years: like, who wrote it, why each book was written, who decided what books would be included, what books and verses were forgeries, and the differing theologies of each Bible book writer.

The Roficks were ripe for the picking and easily snookered by experts who knew how to take scriptures out of context. JWs are masters at giving people the impression that their group—and only their group—knows the Bible, that God reveals Bible truths exclusively to JWs.

Childhood as a "True Believer"

For the children of parents who decide to become JWs, there are no options. And so, Mariuca was never asked if she wanted to be a member. She was five years old and had no say in the matter. But as a child, she also had no trouble believing JWs had the truth, because that's what her parents believed.

She was taught to believe that Jehovah God directed the men who set policies and rules for all JWs. And she believed that God would protect her at Armageddon if she followed all the rules. Being a good JW, she didn't experience the angst that many kids have because they think they're not worthy of God's protection when He kills billions of non-believers at His great day of vengeance, Armageddon.

In fact, Mariuca was a relatively happy child with only occasional bouts of typical JW inflicted guilt, phobias and depression, and she was a true believer.

Mariuca also became an expert at *JW loaded language*. If someone didn't like going to the meetings or in the door-to-door work, "they didn't love Jehovah." If members stopped going to the meetings, "they were falling out of the truth."

If a person was thinking about going to college, she thought, "Armageddon is only a year or two away. Why would they want to do that?"

If some JWs decided they didn't want to be members any longer, Mariuca believed that "extreme shunning is a loving act to help bring them back to their senses."

I asked if she was ever bothered by the fact that only men had leadership roles in her congregation and at JW headquarters. She said that hadn't been a problem because her writing, speaking and people skills were utilized and appreciated by the men in authority. She was praised for being a "hard worker."

Then I asked if the Watchtower's obsessive-compulsive policies on sexual sobriety bothered her? She didn't see it that way as a child. The only thing that bothered her was their position that "only JWs will survive Armageddon." She thought many good people, like most of her non-JW relatives, would be spared.

Other than that, she bought into the Society's lists of "dos and don'ts." If you kept busy—and she kept busy—you are blind to their double standards, inconsistencies, bad science, poorly-thought-out theology and us-against-them mentality. That you are being *unduly influenced* would have never occurred to her.

17

Mariuca at 12 years old

Mariuca was baptized at age fourteen in 1979. As part of the baptism process, she acknowledged the sacrificial death of Jesus Christ, repented of her sins, dedicated her life to doing Jehovah's will, and acknowledged that JWs were "God's spirit-directed organization here on this earth." As bizarre as the latter sounds to her today, she willingly made that vow to God and to those attending her baptism.

She took those vows seriously, and so even while going to high school, she "auxiliary pioneered"—seventy hours of door-to-door canvassing a month—several times a year. She also had an official role at many circuit assemblies.

After graduating from high school, she served as a full-time pioneer while working part-time at a company owned by JWs. At the annual district conventions, she was a secretary in the Chairman's Office.

A New Life at Bethel

When she was twenty-two (and according to her father "not

at all ready"), she married a Bethelite—a full-time worker at the JW headquarters in Brooklyn, NY. Six days after the wedding, she joined her new husband at Bethel, living and working there from 1987 to 1997.

While at Bethel, where Watchtower literature is produced, she worked in the deluxe bindery's shrink wrap department, in the press maintenance department's office and tool crib, and in the pressroom as a proofreader.

Mariuca at Bethel working as a proofreader

During the ten years she lived and worked at Bethel, Mariuca didn't realize that institutionalized living for married couples handicaps their potential for intimacy. It is not a place to be, especially for a newly married couple. That kind of social environment taxes even couples who have been happily married for many years.

To complicate matters, the high-control religion practiced by JWs relegates women to second-class status. And the Society is compulsive-aggressive about enforcing sexual "dos and don'ts" on its members. If a couple ends up sexually compatible, it will be sheer luck.

So while Mariuca was smart and loved her work, she had no idea about the tightrope she walked while living at Bethel—and she was not prepared for the precipitous fall awaiting her.

19

Life at Bethel

So what is life at Bethel like for a married couple? Each person is assigned work by a man, who most likely has no professional personnel training. The male supervisor could even have poor people skills, as his position in the Club's pecking order is a gift from a male hierarchy that believes it is directed by God's spirit.

If the supervisor was employed at a Fortune 500 company, he would be forced to abandon the blatant anti-female sexist personnel policies which are embraced and enforced at Bethel. Otherwise, he would be fired or subjected to never-ending lawsuits.

All new Bethelites are assigned to work in a physically demanding job for five-and-a-half days (forty-four hours) each week. Married couples eat their meals at a pre-assigned ten-person table. They must always sit in the same chair. Only men can sit at the two ends of the table.

For six days a week, Bethelites were required to attend and participate in a 7:00 a.m., 15-to-30-minute morning worship service, followed by breakfast in a room with hundreds of people. For most Bethelites, this meant getting out of bed around 6:00 a.m. to clean up, dress and walk to the dining room. It was like starting your day in a holier-than-thou frat house with no time for intimacy.

All Bethelites are assigned to a congregation in the greater NYC area, at least when Mariuca and I lived and worked at Bethel. (I lived there between 1962 and 1964.) Travel time to and from Bethel can be as long as two hours. Bethelites must attend weekly meetings there, participate in the door-to-door work, and do what is needed to help their congregation prosper.

For the husband, his resume is enhanced if he serves as an elder and gives public talks. There is more, but one can quickly see the strain that this constant working for the Lord and attempting to impress Bethel leaders—trying to prove that you love Jehovah more than the next guy—can have on a marriage.

On December 5, 1994, at 9:30 a.m., Mariuca experienced the biggest shock of her young married life—and she didn't see it coming.

Shattered Dreams—Heartbreak and Heartache

When her husband of seven years said they "needed to talk," she had no idea what he wanted to tell her. Seated alone in their one-room paper-thin-walled apartment, Charley dropped the "F-bomb." He admitted that he had committed "fornication" with one of his Bethel workmates, a married woman. And, this wasn't just a one-night stand.

Yes, he still cared for his wife, but now he really loved his new lady friend, Racey Morris. In fact, Mariuca knew that Racey was a flirt, but going all the way with her husband while living at Bethel—"God's House"—that was a major shock.

It was ironic, because Racey at that very moment was giving her husband the same bad news that Charley was reporting to Mariuca.

No one is ever prepared to get that kind of news, especially Mariuca. She would have described herself as "a happy person" before this happened. She liked her life at Bethel and was totally naïve about how this environment could have contributed to Charley's poor judgment.

She also had no idea of the consequences of the sexually repressive JW policies—policies that clearly spell out what members can and cannot do in their bedrooms. While Charley had roving eyes, had he and Mariuca been better informed about sexual intimacy from a well-trained counselor, this scene might have been avoided.

What Mariuca knew was that Charley had cheated on her, and she was pre-programmed for how to respond and what to do if and when she heard bad news like this. So she told Charley, "Go talk to a JW elder at Bethel and tell him what you've done. He'll know what you need to do."

That's how one is trained to think in an environment which mandates a prompt confession of sexual infidelity for all its members. You must tell an elder, always a man, about your indiscretions and ask for his help. You are forced to get absolution from a man with no marriage counseling training—a man who believes women were created only to love and obey their husbands.

Charley knew the drill well, as he had already done some

serious confessing earlier that morning. But he didn't tell Mariuca about that. He had a plan and he wanted to be in total control of this conversation. So he said, "Yes, I'll do that. I need to confess right away." But then, he suddenly lost control.

Both Charley and Mariuca started crying uncontrollably for nearly two hours. I'm sure that Charley could feel his soon-to-be ex-wife's pain. She was in shock and maybe in total denial of their situation. He was not proud of what he had done, but he needed to bring closure to his first relationship. At least that was his plan. After all, a good cry never hurt anyone.

An hour before confessing to Mariuca, Charley and Racey had jointly admitted their affair to a Bethel elder, sharing all the very personal and sordid details. They probably described how many times they had sex, where and when it occurred, if anyone might have seen them, if oral or anal sex was involved, and whether they were sorry for breaking God's commandments.

Of course we will never know, because what they told the elder was privileged information. In fact, if it had been up to Charley, Mariuca would not have learned about the joint confession.

After he and Mariuca stopped crying, Charley told his wife that he still cared for her and regretted his poor judgment. Unfortunately, he loved his new girlfriend and wanted to be with her. For Charley, there was no chance of reconciliation.

One can only imagine the pain and shock that Mariuca experienced. There wasn't anyone she could talk to. Her world was crumbling, and it was all happening at Bethel. As far back as she could remember, Bethel was the place she wanted to be, like Mecca is to a Muslim. This was the world headquarters for the Creator of All Life, Jehovah God. The best people on the earth supposedly lived at Bethel.

While Mariuca had not thoroughly scrutinized this premise, her fantasy world had supported her needs for the last seven years. She thought she was happy and that her life was good, but now all of this was happening. Soon she would be a "divorcee at Bethel." What would people think of her?

If that wasn't bad enough, she and Charley were required to meet with a three-man judicial committee at Bethel several times over the next two days. Their testimony would be analyzed and scrutinized by elders who would decide Charley's fate and consider the role that Mariuca may have had in holding back from satisfying Charley's sexual needs during their marriage.

"Fair and Balanced"—Facing a Judicial Committee

At the first session held the following day, Mariuca and Charley sat together in front of the three judges—a Watchtower judicial committee meeting. One of the elders wondered if Mariuca should be present while another elder believed it would be better if she heard Charley's testimony. They stopped, excused themselves and went outside to reach an agreement.

When they returned, Mariuca was asked to leave. Later they called her back and asked several personal questions. Over the next two days, Mariuca and Charley were never present together at any of the judicial meetings.

Mariuca remembers how quickly she accepted the decision to have separate meetings as something Jehovah must have wanted. But over the next few months she could not stop thinking about how unfair it was that she was never asked to comment on what Charley may have said about her and their marriage.

In fact, that decision continued to haunt her for many years. It was a small chink in the armor, a tiny leak in the dam, but still she believed JWs had the truth and anyone who was not a JW was controlled by the Devil.

During the two days of interrogation, Charley moved out of their room. But he and Racey were talking with each other like they were a married couple. Racey even called Mariuca's room on one occasion and asked Mariuca if she could speak to him. Mariuca said "no" because the elders told her that Racey and Charley should not be communicating with each other.

While reflecting on that call from Racey, Mariuca asked me, "I wonder what would have happened if I had put down the phone, walked to the elevator, gone up to Racey's room, knocked on her door, and when she opened it, I had punched her in the nose? Would the Bethel elders have simply given me a slap on the wrist?"

She double-winked at me and said in jest, "I bet they would have."

On Mariuca's last meeting with the judicial committee, she was asked if she would take Charley back or if she planned on divorcing him. Mariuca informed them that Charley had been very clear that he loved Racey and wanted to be with her. She asked, "How is this choice actually in my hands?" But still, they needed a decision.

As painful as it was for her, she remembers almost laughing because it seemed the elders could not seriously think she had any real choice. Perhaps she could leave Bethel with Charley and later hope to convince him to stay with her. But she told them that her only reasonable, logical and realistic choice would be to divorce him.

When the judicial meetings concluded, the verdict was unanimous. *Charley and Racey would not be disfellowshipped.* The judges decided they were "sufficiently repentant," and only needed a minor reprimand, although they would have to leave Bethel.

No one normally gets reprimanded that lightly, so the verdict was a big shock to everyone at Bethel.

The decision was an emotionally disturbing blow for Mariuca. What had Charley said that would allow the elders to make that decision? That was not protocol for JWs at Bethel, or anywhere else. Instead, it actually cast suspicion on Mariuca, leaving the impression that Charley had some good reason to be unfaithful.

To add insult to injury, two months after Racey was dismissed from Bethel, a picture of her appeared in The Watchtower magazine. Racey had posed for it before she and Charley confessed. No one seemed the wiser when Racey's image was inadvertently published.

Mariuca was at the Monday night Watchtower Study and carefully placed a song book over the image when that particular page was being discussed. A friend in the Graphics Department knew how offensive Racey's picture would be to Mariuca and called to apologize for the *faux pas*.

I'm sure that story was told many times at Bethel, but only in private. After all, "God's organization" could not possibly make

24

a mistake like that. To suggest anything otherwise would only "bring reproach on Jehovah."

The "Joy of Sex"—or Lack Thereof

Today, Mariuca thinks about the underlying causes for the breakup of her marriage with Charley and is embarrassed, remembering how naïve she was when they were first married, due in large part to the Society's policies related to sex.

"I did not know much about sex other than what I had read in the *Family Book* and *Youth Book*. Only that a man and woman should lie close together, how the man's organ fits into the woman and they derive pleasure from it. It seems impossible today that I could have been so child-like, knowing nothing about sex, let alone my own sexuality. But growing up as a JW, I was forever being warned about Jehovah hating masturbation, sex before marriage, adultery and oral sex.

"'Sex' was a dirty word and, at best, a distraction to pleasing God. If you were strong, you could resist and pretend the sex drive didn't exist. That's kind of how I was. The Watchtower advised men to get married if they 'burned with passion.' (1 Cor 7:9) But it was all about the man. A woman's sexuality and needs were never addressed. For her, 'any port in the storm' will do.

"Anyway, for the seven years we were married, it was all about Charley. I thought I had done my wifely duty. Unfortunately, the magic spark some couples achieve was beyond my reach. So when Charley said he had cheated on me, one of the first things I asked him was, 'Did she have an orgasm?'

"This is embarrassing to admit today, as I thought he had tired of me because I couldn't reach one. And if you're curious, Charley didn't answer my question.

"However, the last thing he said to me before packing and leaving our room at Bethel was, 'Looks aren't everything.' Small consolation, but I've chuckled about that ill-timed comment many times over the years. He just couldn't have his cake and eat it too, and somehow he thought I would be flattered with that parting shot.

"Most of the members in the congregation Charley and I attended in Bedford Stuyvesant appeared to be hurt over the fact that Charley was dismissed from Bethel. Like, 'Oh, we know Charley and Mariuca; we like Charley.'

"The presiding overseer came to Bethel the day Charley left and helped him pack his car for the trip home to Michigan, and his phone number was circulated among the elders and ministerial servants so they could call him. Not one of them said a word to me for several weeks after that."

Mariuca asked for, and was granted, a leave of absence to return home to spend the next three weeks with her family in Detroit. While there, Charley served Mariuca with divorce papers, which was very upsetting to her. Charley didn't waste any time getting the legal mechanics going.

He was in a big hurry so that he could get married and spend bedroom time with Racey, to get through all of the hoops, which JW policy forces on a person so he or she can be "right with God" and His Big-Brother-Is-Watching-You Organization, the Watchtower Society.

When it was time to go back to Bethel, Mariuca was nervous, worrying that she would be met with stares and the subject of gossipers. While JWs claim that gossip is something that is not found among their group, those that "have been there and done that" know better. JWs have turned their style of gossiping into an art form. And Mariuca had already heard several rumors from other sisters, implying that way too many people felt that "she HAD to know something was going on."

The women she shared a locker with at the Factory (all cleaning personnel) were especially kind during her first week back at Bethel. They pooled their money and bought stamps and paper for Mariuca to make greeting cards—a popular activity at Bethel. With the help of her brother Randy, also a Bethelite, several of her friends sneaked into her room and gifted her with a beautiful bouquet of flowers and a "Welcome Back" sign. She was allowed to live in her room without a roommate.

One of Mariuca's close friends introduced her to Judi Dee and explained what happened. A year before, Judi's husband of many years was the cheater, and she the cheated. The husband was quickly dismissed from Bethel, but unlike Charley, he was disfellowshipped.

Judi recommended reading *How to Survive the Loss of a Love*, a book that had helped her. She also arranged for her brother in the legal department to offer Mariuca advice. Shortly thereafter, a Bethel lawyer was assigned to handle Mariuca's divorce.

In his haste to get back into the bedroom with Racey, Charley neglected to do his homework. The divorce papers served on Mariuca were not legal because Charley had not been a Michigan resident for at least sixty days prior to filing. The Bethel lawyer contacted Charley and reported that a New York divorce would have to be filed unless he agreed to pay Mariuca alimony.

However, New York was not a "no-fault" state, so a divorce could easily last years. That meant that all the dirty details would be aired in the pleadings and Charley, being the adulterous party, would be put in a bad position. Being that it was a "no-fault" state, Charley preferred Michigan for his divorce.

Charley didn't have an attorney and called Mariuca right away, complaining that this was "blackmail." Mariuca told him he should talk with her attorney. In the end, Charley paid $7,000 in alimony. The Watchtower's Legal Department did not take a cut from the settlement.

Although $7,000 wasn't a lot of money even then, for a Bethelite it was big bucks. While working in construction at Bethel, Charley learned several trades and those skills allowed him to make extra money on the side. During the years they were married, Charley often made good money in his spare time; money they used for vacations.

So the alimony, while a pittance, was acknowledgement that he owed Mariuca something. By the time he made a lump sum payment more than sixty days had passed. So he again filed for a Michigan divorce, finalizing it in August 1995.

Return to Bethel

Mariuca fondly recalls a sweet memory about something that took place shortly after her return to Bethel. She is 5 feet 9 ½ inches tall, and Charley was only 5 feet 7 inches. So she decided to go shopping and buy some beautiful high heels, later throwing away most of her flat shoes. That event did not go unnoticed by her coworkers and friends.

Mariuca's special gift to herself after the divorce…

Part Two

During her first year of single life, Mariuca requested *shepherding visits*, which is unique to the JW experience. During the *visit* an elder or elders try to encourage a member who might be struggling with the loss of a loved one, be in the early stage of losing their faith, etc. Because JWs are discouraged from meeting with licensed psychologists, these visits are the Watchtower's way of providing pseudo mental health advice, with the elders believing that God's Holy Spirit guides them.

Here's how the visit works: The JW member-in-need requests a meeting with an elder. If granted, one or two elders are assigned to be "shepherds." During the actual visit the problem is identified and followed up with a pep talk peppered with cherry-picked scriptures to make it feel like Jehovah is there working His magic.

Mariuca had several shepherding visits after the divorce, some she requested and others were initiated by elders in the pressroom where she worked. She always thought they were helpful, because the elders were compassionate and caring. But not one of the shepherding elders was properly trained to evaluate Mariuca's mental state. While their efforts were well-intentioned, they were actually setting her up for a major breakdown. It was only a matter of time.

What helped Mariuca was working long, hard hours every day. Interacting with a hundred men in the Bethel Pressroom each week didn't hurt. And during lunch time, she enjoyed playing cards with her brother, Randy. The two of them also partnered and played Bid Whist in the evening, giving her the opportunity to meet interesting single Bethelites in a relaxed environment. And that's when it happened. The guy's name was Lewis.

When it became obvious that Lewis wanted a boy-girl relationship, Mariuca didn't like it. She recalls a conversation with her brother Randy. "Guess who had the NERVE to call me after a card game, trying to sweet talk me?"

After she reported who it was, they both laughed. Lewis was six years younger than Mariuca, and from the neck up he was "one homely dude," as an outspoken aunt once described him.

But not everything was negative about Lewis. He was an excellent public speaker. And from the neck down, he could have passed for a male model, and he was tall. In fact, he was much taller than Mariuca, which she liked.

After rejecting several of his initial requests for a date, she finally gave in and said "yes." As it turned out, Lewis liked doing fun things and was not the "stick-in-the-mud" that Charley was most of the time. Lewis could make Mariuca laugh, liked Bid Whist, and while they roller skated, she felt like she was dancing with a star.

A New Love

Suddenly, it was not about his outward appearance. Lewis doted on her, dining and spending time with her whenever he could. She found him fun to be around. When he finally asked her to go steady and said he wanted to marry her, she was ready. When a friend teased her about his looks, saying that if they ever got married that it would be the "Beauty and the Beast," Mariuca no longer cared.

When single Bethelites start dating, it's protocol to report this activity to the elders of the congregation they attend. And so, in the winter of 1996, Lewis met with two elders at his assigned Hall. He informed them that he was dating Mariuca and they were talking about getting married in the spring.

He also told them that he was impressed that she had stayed at Bethel while going through a divorce, that she had overcome much adversity. While he had a low opinion of Mariuca's ex-husband, he let the elders know that Mariuca had never said a bad word about her ex.

Lewis was convinced they would make a good couple because he had worked in the same department with Mariuca for several years. For him, or so he thought, this was not a "fly-by-night" fling.

Both elders listened carefully and offered their best wishes. However, one of the elders, Marshall Macon, a man who saw himself as a "big brother", asked if they could speak privately. When they were alone, Marshall let Lewis know that he was very disappointed; Lewis should have confided with him before he started dating Mariuca. He felt she was not a good match, Lewis was too naïve about women and should have investigated what went wrong with her first marriage.

However, Marshall told Lewis not to worry, as he planned to talk with Mariuca to see what he could glean about the breakup. And because Marshall fancied himself to be a spy for a good cause,

Mariuca would not know what precipitated the conversation, at least that's what Marshall thought.

Marshall called Mariuca and scheduled a meeting. In hindsight she realizes that agreeing to meet with him was a bad decision. For early in their one-on-one, two-hour conversation, she realized Marshall was interrogating her, trolling for reasons why Charley was unfaithful and why she and Lewis would not be a good match.

Marshall had one very long talk with Lewis after speaking with Mariuca, warning Lewis that he was making a huge mistake. Marshall even suggested that Lewis talk with Charley to get his side of the story. And of course, Mariuca was not to be told about any of these conversations.

Marshall's efforts appeared to have little impact, as Mariuca and Lewis were married on April 5, 1997.

A Heartbreaking Discovery

However, the marriage was not three weeks old when Lewis started playing the "I'm-not-going-to-talk-to-you" game, executing the silent treatment like an expert. The first two times it lasted for only a day. But on the third try, he held out for three days without saying a word to her.

After the three-day episode, Mariuca was very concerned. Each time it happened again, she'd beg Lewis to tell her what was wrong and get no response. But, one time after asking "What's wrong?" she noticed he wrote something in a notebook.

Later that day, while putting the laundry away, she saw the notebook in their chest of drawers. Lewis wasn't in the room, so she picked it up, thinking she'd find a clue as to why Lewis believed he needed to give her the silent treatment.

She opened the notebook and read his last entry, "I have made a huge mistake. I should have never gotten married." Mariuca dropped the notebook on the floor and gasped. Her head was spinning, now feeling quite nauseated.

When Mariuca saw Lewis later in the day, she confronted him immediately. But as soon as he figured out that she had been snooping in his notebook, he went into a hissy fit, shouting that she had no business reading something so personal.

She responded with, "But you wrote in it, right in front of me, when I tried to get you to talk with me this morning. What are you trying to say?"

That's when he confessed his true feelings. The marriage was a huge mistake. He wasn't ready for a longtime relationship with Mariuca. They were mismatched. "Getting married to you was a bad idea. I wish I'd listened to Marshall's advice."

Mariuca was devastated with the news and for days she couldn't block it out of her mind. She thought of herself as unlovable—just a big fool. Her decision-making skills were flawed, as was the chemistry between her and her husband. And it had all happened so quickly. Why hadn't she waited and dated more guys?

She was depressed and distraught, feeling that life wasn't worth living. Suicide appeared to be only way out—not a rational response—as Mariuca confesses today. But her world was crumbling. She felt so alone—an outcast—a woman no man could possibly love. And there was no one she could talk to except Lewis.

In June, Mariuca actually went through the motions, thinking she could end her life in a bathtub located in a private bathing room in her hallway. But she was unable to make it happen. Sick with guilt, she told Lewis about her failed suicide attempt.

He suggested talking with the Bethel doctor, which she did on several occasions. It helped, but her depression didn't go away.

It galls me to know that Mariuca's depression was mainly due to Watchtower's invasive culture of undue influence, which is a methodical system of control that Watchtower uses to manipulate the thoughts and emotions of its members. A good mental health therapist would have diagnosed Mariuca's problem immediately, and this is one of the reasons Watchtower demonizes therapists and psychologists.

Several months later, Lewis met with the Bethel Factory Overseer, Homer Myway. Homer had heard about Mariuca's suicide attempt, and told Lewis straightaway that he and Mariuca were no longer welcome at Bethel. They had to leave.

Lewis knew that framing their departure as a consequence of the suicide attempt was not a good idea. It would only worsen Mariuca's condition. So instead, Lewis told her that to salvage their marriage, they needed to leave Bethel and move closer to her family in Detroit, which they did in October 1997.

Back home in Detroit, both Mariuca and Lewis started working full-time. The money was good, but it did not improve their relationship.

On June 15, 1999, Mariuca penned in her diary, "Last Sunday I was browsing in a bookstore looking for a good book to read, something to help me to understand the whys and hows of my relationship…

"My life has taken some unexpected twists and turns, because I have less than the best judgment when it comes to choosing men. I am easily swayed by the things they say to me, and I fail to notice if what they say and what they do matches.

"However, in my current relationship there were many warning signs during the courtship. I only wish I had the good sense to heed them. Now I'm in the awful position where I have to, or I feel that I have to, get out of the relationship to save my heart and soul. Or just stay and take my chances in a situation I'm not emotionally equipped to handle.

"I don't have the strength to stay or the strength to leave. What can I do? I have tried to end my life. I have tried to act as if nothing is wrong and I'm vulnerable to other men who give me attention.

"My family is self-absorbed. When I was in a psychiatric ward last year, after my second suicide attempt, I was there for two weeks. My husband came to see me four times. My parents were no-shows the whole time."

A Judicial Split Decision

A year after writing those thoughts in her diary, Mariuca discovered that Lewis was involved in an extramarital affair. When she confronted him, he apologized and agreed to meet with JW elders at a judicial meeting to confess. He was sorry and assured everyone that it wouldn't happen again.

Because Mariuca decided to forgive him, Lewis was not disfellowshipped. But two months later, Lewis moved out of the house and said he wasn't coming back. They were divorced in October 2001.

This created a big problem for Mariuca. Because she had accepted him back after he had been unfaithful, per JW policy, she was not "scripturally free" to date again. So Mariuca located Lewis' mother and asked for help. She convinced Lewis to write and send a confession letter to Mariuca stating that she was free to remarry.

In 2002, the elders at the Kingdom Hall she attended were asked to review the confession letter. Mariuca needed them to okay the legitimacy of Lewis's letter so she could start dating again. Unfortunately, it was a split decision. Two of the elders approved it, while a third elder decided Mariuca had forged the letter.

Because they could not reach an agreement one way or the other, the matter was turned over to men higher up in the pecking order at Bethel, in Brooklyn, NY.

After a year with no communication about her appeal, Mariuca was finally given the green light to date again. For her it was a shallow victory because by then she realized that she was allowing ridiculous and arbitrary rules from old men, not God, to guide her life.

A Complete Physical Breakdown

On February 1, 2003, Mariuca started feeling very ill. Muscles in her shoulders, upper legs and pelvic area began to ache; the pain gradually getting worse every day. This lasted for two months. Then the elders came to see her, wondering why she hadn't been attending all the meetings and going door-to-door.

She told them about her symptoms; that she was exhausted, depressed and unhappy with her life.

Instead of recommending a good doctor, they said she "was precious in God's eyes." What she needed to do to get better was to immerse herself in helping others find the truth, read more Watchtower literature, and go to all the meetings.

When Mariuca could no longer walk, dress, or shower on her own, she was taken to a doctor, and diagnosed with "polymyositis"—a chronic inflammation of the muscles extending from her shoulders down to her upper legs.

On April 15, 2003, Mariuca was hospitalized and not able to take care of herself, an invalid at age thirty-eight. While no one could know for sure, Mariuca's doctors suspected her polymyositis was caused by stress.

When she was finally discharged from the hospital, she lived with her parents for three months. But they were too busy to care for her properly. For them, going to meetings and pioneering took precedence. So Mariuca was transported back and forth in a wheelchair between an aunt and her parents. It would take seven months before she could eventually take care of herself and work full-time again.

This seven-month period, feeling gravely ill and totally dependent on others, was the lowest point in her life. At the same time, it taught her something about her real worth to most of her family and friends: for them her needs were clearly a distant second to their field service and meeting attendance, symptomatic of Watchtower's undue influence.

While Mariuca was sick, she requested several "shepherding visits" and those visits proved to be her lifeline. An elder "shepherd" who helped her most was a man named Carl Wilson.

Carl was also one of two elders who met in 2002 to decide if she was free to remarry. He clearly remembered what went on in his mind before, during and after he participated in that judicial hearing.

Carl Shares His Account of Events

Carl's eyewitness account, which follows, is a sobering reminder of how badly Mariuca had been treated by an organization of men who took no responsibility for their unjust policies and decisions.

In Carl's words, "I worked with Mariuca at a Witness-owned company for two years (1983 and 1984) before she went to Bethel. She was nineteen and I was twenty-eight. So I could see a big change in her, from then to now (2002).

"I thought the poor girl was a horrible victim and I could not believe what had happened to her at Bethel.

"The powers-that-be decided her fate, scammed by her first husband. Their interest in her was very superficial, like 'JW shepherding calls' are going to help someone who should be talking to a qualified psychologist.

"Then, she chooses a flake for a second husband, whom you don't want to know about. He could not make decisions on his own, relying on an egomaniacal Bethel elder who felt the need to meddle in people's private lives.

"Now, she is getting ready to be victimized again by another group of men, who don't know her from a hole in the wall when she asks if it is okay to date again.

"My opinion was that the choice to remarry was hers. This decision was based on my understanding of Watchtower articles, which indicated she was answerable to Jehovah, and the congregation should stay out of it. I had shared my research with the presiding overseer and he concurred. We were the two elders appointed by the body of elders to look into the matter."

When I asked Carl how it happened that there was a split decision, he said, "As a courtesy to the other elders, we shared our findings. That's when all hell broke loose. Gunther Bemis, a real piece of work if ever there was one, inserts himself into the case, raising questions about the confession's authenticity.

"Bemis, a tall, white-haired, generous donor to the Hall, disfellowshipped twice, had real issues with women, thinking it was not a separation-worthy offense if a man slapped his wife with an open hand. Mariuca was present when he reported this revelation while he conducted a congregation book study meeting. Other women were in attendance, and they simply looked at each other realizing there wasn't a thing they could say or do about it.

"Well, Bemis gets this burr up his butt and asks how we know it's the real deal, Mariuca probably forged the letter. He starts telling us about Jehovah's love, how we have to earn it and what women will do when they're desperate. Pure nonsense, but this guy is a rogue elder, lots of them in the organization. The love of power is more important to them than the power of love.

"So because of one dissenting vote, the matter was turned over to elders at Bethel.

"What made the Bemis story even more galling is that Bemis fancied himself to be a handwriting expert, carefully inspecting several documents written by Mariuca along with the Lewis confession. I suspect that he had watched too much CSI and so rendered the following verdict: 'She is conning the congregation.'"

In fact, there were many details related to Mariuca's confession that Carl will never forget. And that information turned out to be life-changing for him.

In Carl's words, "I don't think anyone ever understood how earth-shaking it was for me when I figured out what had really happened to Mariuca at Bethel. The ruling junta chose to believe her first husband's spin on why he was unfaithful, and he got away with murder. But I need to backtrack to tell the story properly.

"A few months before I was asked to evaluate Mariuca's second husband's confession letter in 2002, I had just completed a wasted weekend in elder training. I hated those so-called special schools. We spent way too much time getting lectured on 'rooting out evil' in the congregation; especially in the form of the bad guys who schemed to do away with a marriage in order to acquire a new wife.

"It was made crystal clear that we would have to have ALL THE FACTS. We were instructed to always advise the branch of such cases. There would be no way a claim of repentance could be accepted if the offender left the innocent party and married his partner in crime.

"When Mariuca told me that she was not allowed to be present at the judicial meeting to cross-check her husband's story, I suspected a cover-up—a cover-up that high-ranking Bethel elders knew about and chose to look the other way.

"This was the first time I allowed myself to think that this was not the way God would operate. Once the door to that thought was opened, it allowed me to acknowledge other faults in what I had, up until then, thought was the truth.

"Mariuca also had no idea that a letter followed her around to each congregation she attended, a letter that I had seen. It was a letter from a congregation in the Detroit suburbs, featuring her first husband's twisted version of events.

"Basically, it stated that Mariuca was fragile, emotionally unstable, and implied that she may have been frigid, and would require much shepherding. This letter greatly influenced the infamous Gunther Bemis.

"I considered the letter highly prejudicial—insulting at best—and slanderous at worst. I was saddened that any well-meaning, unqualified-to-counsel, sexist elder would have access to this kind of information, which could most likely complicate the poor girl's life even more than it already was.

"It didn't matter what Mariuca thought or said. The good old boys went in the back room and worked things out among themselves so that a 'good man' could keep serving Jehovah zealously, this time with a 'more suitable partner.'

"That attitude made me think of a case I worked on in a downtown Detroit congregation. Kim, a pioneer sister, contacted her brother-in-law, and my fellow elder, Art Smack, telling us that she had been the victim of repeated physical and emotional abuse. Days earlier, her husband, Rankin, drop kicked her across the room. If you've ever watched professional wrestling or a martial arts movie, you know this is no joke if it happens to you.

"Art and I called on the couple in their home. Rankin readily admitted that he physically abused his wife. But he became irate and emotional to the point of scaring me. This man was obviously unstable. He was crying and screaming at the top of his lungs. He called his wife every foul four-letter word you could think of and constantly referred to her as 'this b****' or 'this c***.'

"I was shocked to say the least. I never expected this good-looking couple who attended all the meetings at the Hall, a pioneer and ministerial servant, had this crazy mess going on in their home.

"Art, who took the lead in this shepherding call, finally tired of Rankin's ranting and raving, and corrected him, saying 'How dare you show disrespect to two elders in the congregation? How dare you disrespect Jehovah after we opened our discussion in prayer?' Never mind that his wife was a human punching bag, who he regularly slapped, kicked, and called her everything but her name.

"This is what I thought about when I first read Mariuca's

introductory letter to our congregation. I knew this attitude was prevalent among elders and most men in the congregation, and an attitude that would unjustly complicate Mariuca's quest for happiness in life.

"I'm happy to say that believing her story, while it took me awhile, *was my first step out of the cult and finding **real** truth.*"

Part Three

For three years from 2002 to early in 2005, Carl, always with another elder, helped shepherd Mariuca, giving her balanced advice. When sick with polymyositis, Carl, along with another elder, visited with her regularly. Even after partially recovering, she enjoyed going in the door-to-door service with Carl's family because they worked at a slower pace and took it easy on her.

During one conversation with Carl, he privately told Mariuca that he was seeing a therapist. This was a shock because she knew most JWs frowned on going to mental-health counselors. At the same time, it was comforting news. It was also the spark that gave her the courage to look for and hire a reputable therapist who ultimately helped her identify several key issues.

A Chance Event

Once during the summer of 2005 after going door-to-door, Mariuca was riding in a car with Carl, his wife and their seventeen-year-old daughter, Maggie. During the course of one conversation, Mariuca asked, "If you don't have your mind, what have you got?" She was thinking about her relationship with her schizophrenic and paranoid grandmother, wondering if she might eventually become just like her.

The next day, after the Sunday morning meeting, the four of them decided to chat about Mariuca's comment. Suddenly, Carl's wife mentioned that Carl suffered from depression and how debilitating it was for him when it happened. This news came as a big surprise to Mariuca. Carl had been a big help to her over the last three years. Who would have guessed he was struggling with depression?

Suddenly it occurred to her that she might have offended him and wanted to apologize, but felt constrained there at the Hall. Instead, she decided to send Carl an email message to try to make amends.

Mariuca knew his email address because Carl sent email messages weekly to members at the Hall; it was his way of helping them prepare for the Sunday Watchtower Study meeting. He was the "Study Servant" in charge. Other than that, she had no idea of what Carl's personal life was like or his current mindset.

Living Two Lives

Carl appeared to have everything under control as he was a caring, committed elder. Mariuca did not know he was living two lives. He and his wife were totally mismatched, had not slept together in years and their home life was living hell.

Carl's wife was forever putting him down; he was never good enough for her. But among fellow JWs, they played the game "all is well." That was not uncommon, because according to JW rules, they could do nothing about their bad marriage. They would have to tough it out until the new world; then God would make the marriage whole.

So Carl spent most of his free time away from home to escape the hostile environment. Serving as an elder had helped his self esteem, but that too was nearing the breaking point.

Carl was now beginning to question several JW policies, the most offensive being how Witnesses treat women as second-class citizens. Other questionable policies for him related to blood transfusions, not reporting child sexual abuse and domestic violence to the police, shunning, the hypocrisy of elders, and JWs being told to lie and deceive ("theocratic warfare") by the body of elders in Brooklyn, New York.

Carl could also see that Mariuca was someone just like himself. She was a thinker trying to find her way in an insecure world – although she was not yet able to see the "emperor's new clothes" for what they were. She had been beaten and knocked around by JW male chauvinists.

He had been powerless when he had been part of a committee, a body of elders, where only one scoundrel could trump common sense. He was ashamed of his role in telling Mariuca that she was not free to date and remarry. While he did not know how and when, he committed himself to finding a way to help Mariuca.

Carl also knew what depression and mood swings were like. It was part of his life story. He recognized Mariuca as a kindred spirit and a person, like himself, trapped in a world of high-control religion, not yet knowing how to escape.

Carl had also begun to think that many JWs were nothing more than modern-day "Stepin Fetchits"—no matter what their skin color was—turned into religious bigots, dumbed-down stereotypes of people unable to think for themselves and gullible followers, who were too lazy or scared to research JW history, doctrines and policies.

They just believed whatever the Society told them to believe. While many were intelligent, they were willing to play the role of Watchtower lackeys, simply doing anything the Society told them to do.

While that's what Carl thought, he was not yet aware of the social dynamics of undue influence and how Watchtower uses it to enslave the minds of members.

A Sudden Change in Carl

About three months before, it suddenly dawned on Carl that he and Mariuca were traveling on the same bumpy road together and that road was heading in a totally different direction from everyone around them.

Carl was intensely aware that Mariuca accepted him for who he was, warts and all. She laughed at his jokes, and she was an active, attentive listener whenever he had something to say.

Mariuca had recuperated nicely from her debilitating illness and was getting expert advice from her therapist. In the process, a rose was beginning to blossom. She was turning into a vibrant, attractive woman. No one else seemed to see it, but Carl did. Wow! Mariuca was a beautiful woman, and she was someone just like himself, someone who had been kicked around and underappreciated all her life.

Seeking a Different Direction

Carl didn't want to be a Jehovah's Witness any longer, not yet knowing how he could make it happen. However, he began for the first time to imagine Mariuca as someone he could leave with, although that was probably just a dream.

He wasn't the type who looked for one night stands; he had never cheated on his wife. So how could he tell Mariuca what was rumbling in his head?

Mariuca had no idea that Carl was running on a spiritual treadmill going nowhere. She didn't know that he was planning to jump off, or that he was looking at her as his potential run-away partner. In fact, Mariuca thought she might have offended him when she said, "If you don't have your mind, what have you got?"

In September 2005, Mariuca wrote the following email: "Carl, I enjoyed working with you and your family in service yesterday. It means a lot to me. You hold a special place in my heart because if it weren't for your shepherding, friendship and attention, I would very likely not be an active member of the congregation.

"This morning after the meeting, you mentioned that the brothers encouraged you in your bouts of depression, saying you should not to step down because of it.

"I want to tell you that you are a gem of a brother and it would be a disservice to the congregation if you could no longer serve. You have been a great help to me. Your willingness to go beyond the superficial is one thing that makes you special.

"When your wife talked about your depression, I felt bad and wanted to cry. I want only the best for you and to be a part of your support system when it is appropriate. I have a support system for my polymyositis and I imagine you have one too."

The next day, Carl responded. "Mariuca, what a marvelous letter you composed!

"I have found the world too full of selfish, uncaring people. Too many times it becomes discouraging to the point of being unbearable. Some actually take pride in being cold and aloof. So many people are incapable or afraid of expressing true emotion and kindness. Sadly, that is what is needed most.

"My depression and mood swings can be compared to seeing life through the darkest of glasses. At times when the glasses are removed, the light is so bright and intense that suddenly you see the world as totally wonderful. You feel smarter, faster, better than anything, even indestructible, unstoppable. The problem is that invariably you crash, worse than any car crash. If you're pulled free from the aftermath, you still want to die. And the rollercoaster ride continues. That's how I've lived my life, on that rollercoaster, for more than thirty years.

"Never could I have imagined that someone as sensitive, kind, considerate and tall as you could ever dream of associating with someone as small as me. At least that's what I used to think. You have shown me, and I believe you, that I am as tall as anyone. But remember, I am still a crude work in progress.

"I have always seen you as a great beauty outwardly. Now I realize your inner beauty eclipses what is physical. You are so humble, so clean, and so wise. I do understand how tender your heart is and I hope that does not make you cry. I now conclude this letter with the words of a brilliant poet, EnVogue, 'If I could wear your clothes, I'd pretend I was you.'"

Carl's response was not what Mariuca expected. It was a side of Carl she had never seen. Like a big breath of fresh air it was exhilarating, very exciting to get that kind of attention when your self-esteem is near rock bottom. Despite her confused state of mind—and never in her wildest dreams—could Mariuca have ever imagined how this story would eventually play out.

Okay, maybe Carl knew…

• • •

Like it or not, what follows is the core substance of a remarkably unconventional love story.

Before making any moral judgments, I ask the reader to remember that Mariuca and Carl's story did not take place under normal circumstances. Mariuca and Carl were trapped in a high-control non-benevolent religious group that is adept at unduly influencing its members. Members who actually believe the leaders of the Watchtower Society are directed by a Higher Power—God Himself—and critical thinking skills are a liability. So please remember this as you continue reading.

Recognizing the Realities of Undue Influence

Before I continue with the rest of the story, the reader needs to know that at this point in time both Mariuca and Carl were seeing "cracks in the dam." That their religion may be another Wizard of Oz. That it could be a make-believe fantasy world, with followers willing to sacrifice happiness and normality for the promise of everlasting life, a promise from Watchtower for which it is not held accountable.

In other words, if Watchtower is wrong about eternal life for all good-standing JWs, what can someone do about a worthless promise from their grave?

But, when you, your family and friends are being unduly influenced by the same high-control religious group, it is not easy to break away. If one says they are no longer a believer, their JW parents, children, siblings, and other relatives will shun them and pretend they do not exist. For that reason, they must first decide if it is even possible to leave, and if so, then carefully plan their exit.

Carl was near his breaking point. He saw firsthand the heart-wrenching damage caused when JW elders "cherry pick so-called Bible principles" as they meddle in people's lives. He watched first hand, as elders foolishly tried to mentor repressed and sexually ignorant men and women.

One incident had proved particularly troublesome for Carl: A young man named Sam, who was obviously gay, had been persuaded to believe that God wanted him to live like a real man and to like girls. A so-called "loving" elder took Sam under his wings and started teaching him how to "be a man." The elder even went so far as to pick out a lovely young sister for Sam to date. Like a sheep, Sam did what the elder told him to do.

Unfortunately, trusting "sheep-like" Sam was devastated when he discovered that he was HIV positive. He realized that he would have no one to love for the rest of his life. After he had confided his situation to his mentor, the "consoling" elder told Sam, "Jehovah lets us reap what we sow" and "He won't save us from our sins." Then he let Sam know that he would be alone for the rest of his life.

So how did Sam respond to that elder's insights? He went home and killed himself.

Carl shamefully recalls his participation on judicial committees made up of lecherous older men who required sweet misguided young women to relate in detail everything involved in their "immoral sexual acts." During one meeting, when the questioning became so ridiculously intrusive, Carl asked for a "timeout."

During the timeout, the elder asking most of the voyeuristic questions vehemently confirmed his position, saying those questions were "absolutely necessary in order for him to judge her repentance."

When the judicial committee reconvened, that same elder asked the pretty woman, "Did your lover perform oral sex on you? Did you like it?"

Unhappy at Home

Carl was also trapped in a very bad marriage, but according to JW rules there was little he could do about it. His wife was oblivious to Carl's emotional needs, and whenever he suffered from depression, she badgered him even more. Being at home with her was not a peaceful experience.

To make matters worse, the elders at his Hall frequently told him, like a broken record, that his problems were related to his "lack of love for Jehovah."

Carl wanted out, and he saw Mariuca as someone who might share his feelings. However, he decided to take time to test his intuition, to see if Mariuca was willing to leave with him.

Mariuca too was thinking about leaving, but she hadn't discussed her feelings with Carl. Like other JWs, she would have to keep those feelings secret because "Big Brother Watchtower" is ever present. If a true-believing Witness heard that another Witness was losing faith, they often snitched that kind of information to an elder.

If someone innocently made a remark that he or she was unhappy with some JW policy, they'd find themselves the "accused in a Watchtower Kangaroo Court." It's that constant fear of being disfellowshipped and abandoned by friends and family that keeps many JWs from confronting bad policy and/or leaving the organization.

In November 2004, Mariuca wrote in her diary, "I have been a very angry woman for the past few days. Actually, I may be more sad than angry, but I just don't want to let loose and cry. For the past ten years I've been stuck. I suffered a loss of love and my faith, and I don't think that I have ever properly dealt with either.

"I'm a 'refugee,' just going through the motions, barely surviving, but I lost something back there. My mind knows there's probably no other satisfying viable alternative, but it's so hard being present at the Hall when my heart isn't there."

Mariuca found herself trapped in a state of mind that "there's probably no other satisfying viable alternative." She was wrong in making that assumption, but that is what happens when you have been unduly influenced by a high-control religion.

While she did not know it at the time, it would be Carl who would open the door that would allow her to see there was a viable alternative.

Carl and Mariuca Share Their "Secrets"

Mariuca and Carl exchanged several eye-opening emails before they decided to meet for a personal conversation at Panera Bread on September 6, 2005. Carl told her about his recent suicide attempt and subsequent hospitalization. He also shared information about the emotional and financial issues that precipitated it. Then he told her about his "loss of faith."

When it was Mariuca's turn to tell her story, she shared things she had never told anyone. For both of them, it was therapeutic to talk honestly without fear of being judged or told that "they didn't love Jehovah enough." That was a moment in time when they realized they were soul mates. They were forging a strong bond, which would lead to their eventual freedom.

Mariuca learned for the first time that Carl did not have a support system. He was running on autopilot. Mariuca was a new beacon of light in his life, someone who listened nonjudgmentally. Carl was drowning and Mariuca was the life preserver.

During subsequent meetings and conversations, Mariuca felt a special connection with Carl, call it "love" if you will, and he reciprocated. At the time she thought it was platonic and told an aunt that he was the "big brother" she'd always wanted.

But Mariuca also remembers the moment in time, after reading several articles on the subject, when she realized that she was involved in an emotional affair and felt she had to end it. With that on her mind, she called Carl and told him that they had to meet and talk.

The meeting occurred at an Applebee's restaurant. Mariuca told Carl that it was not right for them to be so close, that they needed to end the one-on-one meetings and email conversations. It seemed strange saying that because she hadn't really thought of them as a couple.

He listened and agreed to end the relationship. But Mariuca needed to know that he had written a poem about her. He would email it to her if she would read it, saying the poem ended with the line, "I'm willing to burn." Mariuca agreed to read it.

The next day Mariuca received the following poem:

Inside You

Your soft brown eyes

silent

glances

pause

and flutter,

hesitate.

Unbelievably dark long lashes

slowly

close

and open

inviting me inside.

I advance

unsure.

Touch,

breathe; deep, deeper,

wander inside you and

wonder if you feel

this reckless heat

that guides me to your flame so easily that

I'm willing to burn.

As Mariuca confesses, "My attempt at ending our 'emotional' relationship had not, in fact, been successful. While Carl's devotion was flattering, his openness forced me to accept the gravity of the situation. I wanted him to stop talking! I wanted to express my thoughts, to tell him what was stirring deep within me. So in my email response, I shared the following dialogue from the movie, "The Village":

Ivy Walker: "When we are married, will you dance with me? I find dancing very agreeable. Why can you not say what is in your head?"

Lucius Hunt: "Why can you not stop saying what is in yours? Why must you lead, when I want to lead? If I want to dance, I will ask you to dance. If I want to speak, I will open my mouth and speak. Everyone is forever plaguing me to speak further. Why? What good is it to tell you that you are in my every thought from the time I wake? What good can come from my saying that I sometimes cannot think clearly or do my work properly? What gain can rise of my telling you the only time I feel fear as others do is when you are in harm? That is why I am on the porch, Ivy Walker. I fear for your safety before all others. And yes, I will dance with you on our wedding night."

Mariuca says it was her clumsy way of saying, "Please shut up, I like you, okay?" She thought there were enough layers in the dialogue that he could take it any way he wanted, but he needed to sit back and stop running with this.

She was coming from a background of extreme sexual repression, never thinking there would be a chance in hell that she could actually become sexually involved with Carl, a married man.

Yes, she admits that it sounds bizarre now, but somehow she did the mental gymnastics needed to think she was not going to have what Watchtower calls an adulterous affair, in spite of all the evidence to the contrary.

Carefully Looking for a Change

While Mariuca and Carl were emailing back and forth, she was careful to never write anything she thought would be incriminating. So at some level, she thought she was doing something wrong. She had two failed marriages and was not ready to start another long-term relationship. But Carl was definitely interested in her, and she was intrigued. She enjoyed the conversations with him and was at a point in her life where she did not want to remain a Witness.

She was in a position that if someone came along who seemed like a good person, she would pursue a relationship. She also had a fear of dating someone who was not a Witness. This is a Watchtower-induced phobia that had Mariuca believing that if she married a *worldly person,* that non-JW person would likely be drunk most of the time, probably physically beat her, and be controlled by demons.

On the other hand, she didn't want to be with a Witness. She needed to escape all of the JW guilt and negativity. Only time would tell what sort of relationship she and Carl could have. As Mariuca told me, "I was not committing myself to Carl, but I was willing to give it a try."

Gifts

During "the try" Mariuca moved into her own apartment, with several friends from the Kingdom Hall helping. After she settled in, Mariuca invited everyone over several times for snacks and games. But each time only Carl and his daughter, Maggie, showed up. In this atmosphere, their connections were safe and fun.

After one evening at her apartment, Carl told Mariuca that he had a few house warming gifts he wanted to give her. "Would it be okay to stop over next Friday?"

Mariuca began to worry when Carl did not arrive on time. Two hours late, he finally rang the bell. When she opened the door, he was all alone and dressed like a hip middle-age guy on a date, wearing a new denim jacket, stylish jeans and a snazzy print shirt. Mariuca had no makeup and was wearing her old gray sweats.

When they were alone in the apartment, Carl asked her to go into another room while he set up the gifts in the living room. Mariuca was hoping he had a painting for her because she had just learned he was an artist.

When he announced that he was ready, he asked her to enter the living room with her eyes closed. After guiding her to the right spot, he said she could open her eyes. In front of her stood a huge painting, a picture of Mariuca with a Van Gogh-like background. The painting was stunning, although she winced, as it was not how she would like others to see her on canvas. Carl called it "Girl Interrupted on a Starry Night."

Carl's gift – his painting titled "Girl Interrupted on a Starry Night"

The second gift was a tee shirt screen-printed with the words, "Just your average everyday Sane-Psycho Super Goddess," a line he'd stolen from the song Extraordinary by Liz Phair.

The third gift was a two-CD set of songs compiled by Carl. One CD he called "Mariuca Jazz" and the other "Mariuca Pop." Carl wanted her to play the songs while they sat on the couch and listened.

Mariuca found herself feeling more than a little uncomfortable. "I had this odd mix of excitement and apprehension. I started one of the CDs and sat on the opposite side of an exceptionally long couch and tried to listen. I've never been good at hearing lyrics; so much of it went over my head. We played portions of each song on both CDs and the overriding message was that Carl and I loved each other but we would never be together.

"So I sat there uncomfortably listening. When Carl asked me to join him on the other side of the couch, I moved next to him and eventually rested my head on his chest for several minutes. When the music stopped, he stood up and said that it was time for him to go, but he wanted to know if we could meet for breakfast as he was staying at his dad's house at the time."

An Uncomfortable Romance

"The next morning, I met him at the Original Pancake House in Grosse Pointe Farms. We had breakfast and spent the entire day together, leaving his car at the restaurant parking lot while I drove. We ended up going to the Blue Water Bridge, sitting on a bench looking at the river and talking about what our next steps might be. And I told him that I had not yet made a decision.

"Two years later, I went back to that same bench and took a photo. I wanted to capture what I was looking at while making the most important decision of my life. The picture is called Exodus 2 Genesis. It seemed fitting that I was looking at a bridge, as I was deciding whether I was willing to cross over to a new life.

"I knew that I loved Carl, but up until this point I had always done 'the right thing' and deciding to move forward with a relationship with Carl seemed out of the question. I figured that we had not yet done anything wrong per JW rules.

"However, Carl pointed out that, in fact, we would get in trouble for what had already happened, that it was 'loose conduct.' That unsettled me, as I thought we had not yet crossed any lines.

"That night we went to a made-for-the-movies Italian restaurant across the street from where we had breakfast. We continued talking about what our next steps should be. When I dropped Carl off at his car, he tried to kiss me. But I pulled away, feeling that I needed time to think this oh-we're-going-to-start-kissing thing through.

"There was a television show at the time called 'Cheaters.' In fact you can still see it on TV, where people hire a film crew to follow their mates, who they suspect of being unfaithful. I had watched that show for two seasons—one of my guilty junk-food TV pleasures. The idea of somehow ending up on a Cheaters episode was also playing on my mind when I resisted kissing Carl."

Mariuca spent most of the next day relaxing and chatting with three of her aunts. As they visited, Mariuca's mind was racing, questioning Carl's motives. Did he really love her? Maybe it was a manic phase? Does Carl love me or the idea of me?

She did not think that it was a good idea for someone like Carl, who was in a bad relationship, to be jumping directly into a new one. He needed sufficient time to heal and to understand what he really wanted to do. And, during the following week Mariuca did lots of thinking, but she did it alone.

Carl was frantically sending emails to her for the next few days. He had not heard from Mariuca and he was concerned. Was she okay? He wanted her to say "something" just so he knew she was okay. He didn't want to bug her.

But then….

Three days passed and finally Mariuca was ready for her first response. She composed several emails, but she just couldn't find the right words. She felt overwhelmed, as she had been listening to the CDs that Carl had gifted her. She had gone online and deciphered the lyrics, which had left her smitten and speechless.

When the right words began to flow, it was a fast-paced in-your-face email romance. Finally, Mariuca invited Carl to her apartment on Friday night. They would watch a movie, a comedy, Woody Allen's "Love and Death."

Carl arrived on time and they ordered Chinese take-out. They watched the movie and talked enthusiastically like long-lost friends, and they laughed genuine belly laughs. But it was getting late and still no first kiss. In fact, nothing happened that Mariuca considered "inappropriate."

At midnight, Mariuca felt it was too late for Carl to travel home. He might wake his dad up, as he was staying with him. So she asked Carl if he would like to spend the night at her place. She had a sofa bed and suggested that he could sleep there. (While Carl never reported what went through his mind when he was asked to stay the night, I suspect his dad's uninterrupted sleep would not have made the list.)

While preparing to retire for the night, Mariuca started feeling bad that Carl would have to sleep in the living room. (She now gags when she reflects on her naïve state of mind.) That's when she asked Carl if he would like to sleep in her bed.

"Even at this point," she remembers, "I did not intend to have sex with him. I seriously thought we could sleep side-by-side and maybe spoon, but nothing else would happen. Like in the movie 'Waiting to Exhale,' where Wesley Snipes and Angela Bassett played two very unhappy people who slept the night holding each other while fully clothed.

"So I dressed in drab pajamas which I had slept in the night before. I did nothing that could be considered to be romantic or sexy; that was the extent of my denial. We actually did occupy separate sides of the bed for a while, but one thing led to another and we ended up making love. It was wonderful! Carl was the best."

Mariuca describes her reaction when she first read the last two sentences in the preceding paragraph while we were editing her story. "This made me laugh! It just sounds so funny to me. Honestly, for years later I would tease Carl and say 'JACKPOT!' about that first night because it was a definite first for me.

"The next morning, I woke up without the least bit of guilt about what had transpired—not what I had expected. Since I had been invited to go horseback riding at my aunt's house, Carl and I parted for the day.

"While riding and talking with my aunts, I summoned up the nerve to tell them I'd likely be disfellowshipped very soon. I was involved in a unique relationship, but that's all I'd tell them. Later that evening, Carl joined me at my apartment and stayed overnight.

"The next morning, I woke up with this strong premonition that Carl and I should leave the apartment immediately, like we were about to be ambushed. Of course it was Sunday and normally we'd be going to a JW meeting. And if both of us were not there, it might look suspicious.

"So we headed for Interstate 75, ending up at Coney Island for breakfast. Then it was off to the outlet mall in Birch Run. We shopped, talked and laughed the whole time, a very enjoyable day. We ended the evening eating at a nice Italian restaurant and then back to my apartment.

The Elders Want Answers

"I received a phone call from my ex-roommate sometime in the afternoon, but I did not hear it ring. I listened to the message later that evening, shortly before going home. My old roomie said people at the Hall were asking questions about me. Some of the brothers were looking for Carl.

"Back at my apartment at 9:00 p.m., a light was flashing on the landline phone. It was a voice message from Gunther Bemis who said that he and another brother were outside my door and wanted me to open up. Carl and I sat anxiously together in my apartment, wondering what we should do. We decided to call Gunther at his house and confess.

"Carl called and made small talk at first. Gunther said that he had been at Mariuca's apartment in the afternoon and noticed that Carl's car was parked in the parking lot. Then Carl told him everything.

"That's when Gunther said that what he was hearing—'a JW scandal'—would hit the congregation like a tsunami. A judicial meeting would have to be scheduled as soon as possible.

"I attended the meeting mainly out of courtesy. I thought that I had devoted so much of my life to the Witnesses I should at least go to it. I knew I would be disfellowshipped and I was okay with that, as I planned to continue my relationship with Carl.

"Four elders were at the hearing, and Gunther Bemis was the first to speak. He claimed that Carl and I were in my apartment hiding when he knocked on the door. I said that wasn't true.

"He countered by saying that he saw Carl's car in the parking lot. I explained that we had driven my car and were out of the apartment the whole day. He said I was mistaken. When I asked if he would like to see my receipts for the day, another elder interrupted and asked if Carl and I planned to get married. When I figured out that the subject had been changed, I said 'no.'

"When Gunther asked for a timeline of events, I replied, 'Let's cut to the chase. To stay in the organization, do I need to end my relationship with Carl?'

"The elders said 'yes.' So I told them that I wasn't going to end my relationship with Carl. Then I was told that I would be disfellowshipped, which happened in November 2005."

Sorting Things Out

"Although there have been ups and downs, Carl and I prioritized our relationship. I had to deal with my poor health and being hospitalized on two occasions. Carl was diagnosed in 2011 with prostate cancer. It was rather aggressive, so we decided on a prostatectomy. He had several complications from the treatment; one of them resulted in a serious loss of hearing.

"Then there was the adjustment when you abruptly leave a clannish group like JWs and are shunned by family members and friends. But I learned that Carl was not in some manic phase, that he was devoted to me, as I was to him. What we had been feeling for many months was real.

Wedding photo – 2007

"I am not proud of getting involved with a married man. It still bothers me today, as I know how it feels to be cheated on. Does the end justify the means? It is something that I will struggle with for the rest of my life. I am not proud of leaving the JWs the way I did. But, for many years before leaving, I felt like a refugee. My choices were made under duress, acts of desperation. Carl's love was the best gift that I've ever received, like a warm, fuzzy welcome blanket after years of illness, loneliness and discontent.

"My Aunt Margo's three-word assessment of Carl and me, that we were 'two empty wells,' was very appropriate. It is ironic that JWs are told that they belong to a 'loving organization' when the reality is coldness and emotional distance. Trying to follow JW rules and pleasing elders breeds discouragement, depression, mental illness and chronic illness.

"Now in my relationship with Carl, I am showered with unconditional love and positive reinforcement. He is someone who thinks I am the most special person in the world. I feel very fortunate to have found him. And we were married in Las Vegas on May 1, 2007, one of the happiest days in my life."

A Word from the Author

Writing Mariuca and Carl's story was a very emotional experience for me. I grew up in the same harsh high-control world. Most of my relatives are still JWs and blind to the harm caused by dysfunctional policies, God delusions, and a Big Brother lurking over their shoulder, ready to put the next guilt trip on them.

When you're spoon-fed misinformation on a daily basis and told you will die at Armageddon unless you follow JW rules, even the smartest of people can be dumbed down to become gullible believers. The sexually repressive environment created by JW dogma is oppressive and damaging to adults at any age.

Even today, Mariuca struggles with some guilt, and that hurts me because she is way too kind and smart to have that happen to her. But when a person has been unduly influenced for as many years as she was, there will be some toxic residue, or "ghosts," that will haunt him or her from time to time.

On the other hand, Carl doesn't appear to be haunted by those same "ghosts." Quite different from Mariuca, he describes himself and the love of his life this way: "I was a smart, odd, difficult child who grew into a smart, odd, difficult adult. I had a massive inferiority complex and suffered from depression. Those factors made me ripe for the picking when JWs came along."

Carl Speaks Up

"After seducing me with their talk of a loving brotherhood, they crushed me. My problems were related to 'not loving Jehovah enough.' I was discouraged from seeking professional help. After a suicide attempt in 2005, an elder told me that the only thing I should be doing was resting and going out in field service.

"Mariuca has given me a home filled with love and encouragement. She is my biggest fan and supporter. She believed in my artwork before I did. She teaches me self-confidence. I take some medication when I get really down, but it is her love and devotion that is the medication that sustains me.

"If you asked me to paint a picture of Mariuca," Carl continued, "I would say that physically she's a treat for the eyes. Tall and curvy, and I mean video-game curvy with big dark eyes that suck you in. She has a super bright, a super big smile.

"Mariuca is fifty years old, but looks thirty-five. Looking ordinary and having a wife this hot is a two-edged sword. At best, I have been accused of robbing the cradle—at the worst I have been called her father."

I interrupted Carl and commented that anyone who meets Mariuca will like her and that I'd like for him to tell me why he thinks that's so. He proudly smiled and said, "We've had many a conversation about this. First, people are drawn to her because she is so pretty. It seems most people like to be in the company of beautiful people. Second, she has the ability to engage people to talk about themselves. She's not feigning interest in them. She's genuinely excited to meet new people and eager to listen to them talk about their lives and what they are doing. I think it's one of her ways to make up for all the time she lost fearing wicked, worldly people."

When I asked Carl what life was like for him and Mariuca after leaving a cult, he said, "Life is good. We are busy working artists who always have multiple projects going at the same time. Home is where my heart is. When I was a JW married to my ex, I NEVER wanted to be at home. Home was a sad, scary and dangerous place. The home that Mariuca and I have made is our sanctuary filled with art, love and culture. It's ironic. I commit this 'horrendous' crime, run off with this 'wanton' woman, and finally I get a home that is a haven of rest and peace."

The problem with Carl—well, it's actually a plus—is that when you ask him to say something about himself, he always ends up talking about Mariuca. And I know why. He could not be the person that he has become without her. They are a team, partners, and much better together than they would be alone.

It's easy for him to talk about Mariuca. He told me, "You have to meet her in person to see and feel the joy and thirst for life that this woman radiates. You have to experience her in person to witness the tremendous sensitivity that dwells within her. Words cannot do her justice."

When I asked why Aunt Margo referred to him and Mariuca as "two empty wells", he replied, "She knew how sad both of us were, how kicked around we had been, and how desperate we were for peace." He continued, "I believe I'm one of the luckiest guys alive. I successfully escaped a cult that labored to keep people's minds chained to the ground, covered in the dirt of ignorance.

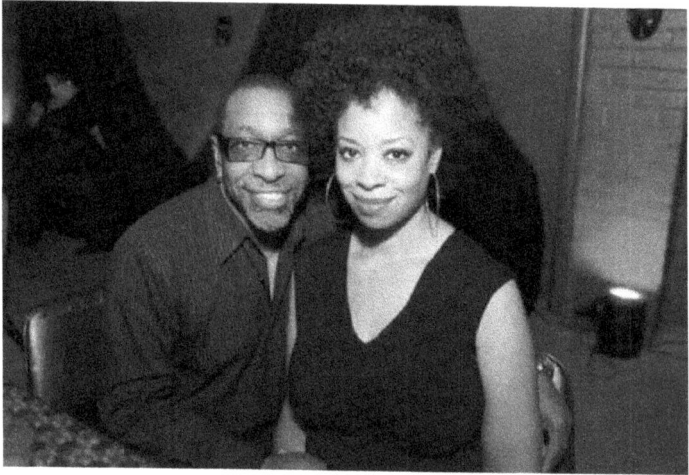

Carl and Mariuca in 2012

"As a JW cult member, I was taught that I, the individual, was of no importance. The only talent worth revering was the talent for making disciples. Now my life is filled with brilliant people who believe knowledge and new ideas are liberating. My friends are artists, writers, actors, educators and activists. And before I forget, I want to thank you, Richard, for writing such a wonderful story about the most wonderful girl in the world."

I suspect that I should let Carl have the last say in this story, but *that ain't going to happen.* I need to say how pleased I am for how well Mariuca's story has come together. I hope that you, the reader, will fall in love with both Mariuca and Carl as much as I have. They've earned it and I'm proud of both of them.

As a consequence of writing Mariuca's story, I feel like a

doting and very happy surrogate father. And Carl is the kind of son-in-law a father could only dream about, if he had a daughter like Mariuca. And yes, there's more…

Mariuca gets the Last Word

"I shouldn't care what JWs think, at least those who once knew me, but I want them to know that I will hang only for the sins I actually committed. That's how I feel sometimes, on my bad days, which are few and far between.

"I'm excited to think that by opening up and allowing Dick to share my midlife 'coming of age' story, it might help others to break free from the chains of JW dependency, where women are treated as second-class citizens.

"I may be a late bloomer, but I'm proof it is possible to leave a high-control religion, find the love of your life, learn the truth about bad JW policies and beliefs, and find real freedom and happiness. So yes, It's Never Too Late!"

An Afterthought:

While Mariuca and I were finishing up telling her story, she asked if I would be amenable to helping her report what it was like to be shunned by family and friends. And so in Mariuca's very own words:

"The best part of sharing my story has been gaining loving surrogate parents. Dick and Helen have been so compassionate and supportive throughout this process. It has been a pleasure getting to know them. Gaining parents who know the world I come from and possess the perspective to understand my missteps and triumphs has been an unexpected benefit.

"I have had abandonment issues as far back as I can remember. Two divorces later, coupled with one disfellowshipping and shunning in the name of God, those issues were still in full force. While my relationship with Carl has healed the wounds caused by my previous marriages, the shunning has taken a great toll on me.

"Most of my family—parents, two siblings and their spouses, both grandmothers, my mother's three sisters—and all of my friends were JWs. Overnight, all of them disappeared without a trace.

"Everyone who I'd grown up with, my former Bethel and NYC friends went into hiding. Not a visit, a phone call, or an email. I recall that during the first few days and weeks after the shunning began how surreal it was when I realized there was scarcely anyone around who I knew for more than a year or two.

"Nothing could prepare me for the trauma of shunning, and it still haunts me at times. It did not help that I wanted to be out of that high-control religion, and even back then I could not imagine returning to it. I no longer believed the things I had been taught and I couldn't bear to have others control my life.

"During those first two years, Carl and I spent our free time together. We loved having our evenings and weekends to ourselves, quality time in our sanctuary.

"But I often thought of my family and it would make me feel sad. I started many letters to family members, trying to explain my reasons for leaving, that I still loved them, but I never completed or mailed any of them.

"When I would see my parents and JW siblings at funerals, I'd have these mild panic attacks, thinking this was a bad dream. Conversations varied from bizarre, disconnected and contrived to almost normal. I could see that the emotional stress was mutual, although I was the leper.

"I struggled with wanting my family to hear my thoughts. I wanted them to know that I was still the same person—I just no longer believed JW teachings. I longed for their acceptance, not on their terms, but on mine.

"I wanted us to be like other families. Yes, we had different religious beliefs. But we peacefully coexisted, mutually respecting each individual's views. I wanted a level playing field, one in which it was conceivable by them that I could actually be a good person, without having the same religious beliefs.

"In those early days I felt like a tree with no roots. I had the sunshine of Carl's love, but there was an entire network of rootstock missing. It took several years, but eventually I felt my roots returning.

"Those roots were based on new relationships where people liked me for me. Carl and I socialized with fellow artists, workmates, former co-workers, ex-JWs, schoolmates and neighbors, meeting some very amazing people.

"Both my grandmothers have died since the shunning began. I've lost two aunts and one uncle. My sister gave birth to a son, with my heart aching to be a part of my nephew's life. But, as the expression goes, 'you can never go home again.' And, after much agonizing and therapy, I am at peace with that for the most part.

"I spend most of my time looking forward. I refuse to spend my freedom nearby my former prison. And so far, I've been rewarded with much more than I could have ever hoped for.

"I'm so grateful that Dick and Helen have come into our lives. I'm looking forward to the joy of seeing all our stories blend together as one.

The End for the Moment

(You can email Mariuca and/or Carl at: mariuca.carl@gmail. com)

Transitioning from Mariuca to Marilyn

There is more to tell about Mariuca, Carl and the special relationship that my wife, Helen, and I have developed with them during the last three years, or at least from when I first met them and learned about their unique story. But, I will share that in a later section of this book.

For now, I want readers to get to know my sister, Marilyn, and to learn why I am so passionate about sharing stories of strong, successful women. Women who have decided to stand up to the Watchtower's *undue influence* and discover their authentic identity, giving meaning and happiness to their lives.

My goal is that Marilyn's story will help us right a wrong and inspire both men and women to work together to make our world a better, safer and more hospitable place to live. Not just for our now, but for hundreds of generations that follow.

Mariuca and Marilyn

Marilyn's Story—Set Up for Failure

I am often asked why I wrote *Growing Up in Mama's Club,* why I blog and why most of my modern-day heroes are ex-Jehovah's Witness Internet vigilantes who aggressively expose the unjust policies of the Watchtower Society. The answer is rooted in Marilyn's Story. First told in *The Ghosts from Mama's Club*, I have rewritten and adapted it so more people can benefit from her story, as follows:

Part One

My sister, Marilyn Kelly, was born September 17, 1948. She was the first of my siblings to have special protection; the kind

Mama believed children earn when they are born, *if* their parents are Jehovah's Witnesses.

Marilyn's conception was also very special. The ritual involved in the process was a gift. It was Mama's way of thanking Papa for capitulating to her wishes. Papa had fought valiantly for over two months trying to keep Mama from becoming a Jehovah's Witness (JW), convinced they were a cult. But when he realized how fruitless his efforts were and would be, he decided to join her. Marilyn was the consequence of that conjugal gift, the living proof of his capitulation.

Marilyn was a drop-dead gorgeous baby, with thick blond hair, sparkling blue-green eyes and an engaging smile. When my parents brought her home from the hospital, I, nearly five, remember how pretty and happy I thought she was. When she turned five, she could pass for a human Barbie doll with her soft, pink-white skin sprinkled with fairy-dust freckles. Mama loved her, but she was Daddy's girl. I think Papa took it personally that he helped produce such a beautiful child.

Marilyn made few demands on our parents. Everyone liked her, and those big beautiful eyes and sweet smile, framed by her bright yellow-blond hair, made it easy for people to remember her name, Little Marilyn Monroe. She didn't cry constantly like our sister Susan did as a baby. Marilyn easily entertained herself and didn't require lots of attention, genuinely enjoying life. Unfortunately, she lacked the sense of curiosity that most kids possess, not certain why, and she had a submissive nature, which made her easy for Mama to manage and mold.

As a teenager, Marilyn's facial complexion was near perfect; so unlike me, who was tattooed with a bumper crop of blemishes. She had no symptoms of bosom-envy cocooning into womanhood. Breast implants would play no role in her life.

Mama kept the boys at a distance with heavy doses of guilt and Watchtower phobias, so Marilyn's hormones played no role in making even one bad decision, as few crimes in Mama's mind came close to sex before marriage.

Unfortunately, Marilyn had one significant handicap. It took her forever to do whatever she had to do or to get to wherever she wanted to go. While she was a very attractive young woman, it turned out to be handicap "number two."

Being "Second-Class"

Marilyn had no trouble learning or accepting the JW "truth" that women are second-class citizens in the eyes of God. Okay, Mama and Marilyn would not have used the words "second class." But if you're a JW, you are taught to believe that God has a pecking order. There's the Big Guy at the top, after Him come angels, and below them are men, below men are women, and then, at the very bottom, there are the animals. Even as a child this didn't make sense to me and I often challenged Mama. Her pat response, as if that helped, was, "Who am I to challenge God and what He says in the Bible? But just remember, He loves us all the same."

The belief that women were a notch lower than men in God's organizational chart impacted almost all JW policy. It was a policy that Marilyn and I easily observed – and one that Mama fully supported. No woman could have a position of authority at Bethel, the headquarters for the Watchtower Society, where JWs are governed. Nor could a woman have a position of authority at the local level, our Kingdom Hall.

At the Hall, it is "men only" for preaching, teaching, judicial hearings and praying. In fact, if there was an official meeting and a woman prayed publicly, she would have to wear a head covering "out of respect for any angels that might be visiting."

I wish I could have told Marilyn and Mama what I know now about the history of religion and its role in minimizing women. In Jesus' time, women were treated like chattel. The Jewish religion supported that view: according to one of the creation stories in Genesis, God created women solely for serving man as a "helpmate."

Building on this sense of second-class citizenship, women were defined as "property" in Exodus. Thus polygamy made sense, for a man could have as many wives, sheep, or cattle as he could afford.

In stark contrast, Jesus was non-sexist. He tried to end discrimination. He had female disciples and traveled and ministered

71

with them. He treated women as equals, breaking the religious rules of his day.

In the six books and verses we know for sure that the apostle Paul wrote, according to most credible Bible scholars, Paul supported an active role for women in the early Christian church. But shortly after he died, the ruling clergy thought this policy was ill-advised and went back to the sexist mentality of the Old Testament.

For much of Western history, women have been relegated to second-class status, with many Christian orthodox churches validating that definition as "God-inspired" and "God-imposed." Because of a woman's lack of size, speed and physical strength, she was relegated to a state of childlike dependency.

In the most basic relationship in human society, the male met his survival needs by claiming that the female's lower status was "God's plan in creation." That way if the woman objected, she had to fight against God as well.

I would have vigorously shared this kind of information with Mama and Marilyn. And to Mama I would have asked, "Was the discrimination of women invented by God or man? Could it be that a select group of men created God in a man's image?" Not that it would have done any good, but I would have felt better.

Most hard-core believers don't want facts. Mama had her version of the truth and it wouldn't change, blind to the damage her truth was having on Marilyn.

To make matters worse, Mama nixed any thought of Marilyn getting a good education or reading non-JW books. Armageddon was imminent; mind you this was in the 1950s. Even if it was delayed and Marilyn reached marriage age before it arrived, she could marry a hard-working JW man. He would be the breadwinner and take care of her, as Papa had done for Mama.

Marilyn didn't need to excel in school. Though smart enough, she was never encouraged to develop her thinking skills as that would breed pride—a Watchtower mistruth and one of the ways Watchtower unduly influenced its members.

Living Without Friends

As a child, Marilyn had no close friends. Perhaps there were kids at school that she met and liked, but to Mama those kinds of kids were "lepers." Worldly kids would get her into trouble. So Marilyn didn't develop the social skills that she would need as an adult.

That was of no concern to Mama, as she knew Armageddon could come any day, it wouldn't be long. All evidence pointed to the end of the world soon, followed by a new paradise world. If Marilyn followed Mama's advice, she would live forever in that new world and have eternity to make many good friends with people who loved Jehovah just like Mama.

Marilyn and I grew up in Los Angeles, California and the few friends we had were JWs. We didn't celebrate birthdays or Christmas, but Mama did organize a special JW "party day" each year where gifts were given and we played games. Mama would invite other JW kids and serve us cake and ice cream; a very special time each year for Marilyn who was by nature a happy person who loved social events.

But there were many unhappy moments for Marilyn and me. One of them was an incident orchestrated by Mama. While at school, I received over twenty Valentine cards, each with a personal message. Those personalized comments made me feel special and liked. But because of Mama's religious beliefs, I knew I should leave these cards at school because Mama told me that Valentine's Day was a "pagan ritual invented by the Devil."

Still, I wanted to show Marilyn the cards and read to her what other kids were saying about me. So I snuck the cards home in my lunch box. When I thought it was safe, I told Marilyn that I wanted to show her something in the backyard. We had looked at maybe ten cards when we heard Mama's voice as she peered out of my bedroom window, "What are you doing?"

When Mama discovered what I was doing—she lost it, going on and on about how bad I was by inviting the Devil into my life. Marilyn was only three at the time and that look of horror on Marilyn's face still haunts me.

It wasn't too long after that when Marilyn and I were playing in the backyard and three neighborhood boys decided to join us. They wanted to know what we were doing. It wasn't that we couldn't talk with our neighbors, but we generally did not play with them for any length of time. One of the boys asked if he could use the swing while another wanted to talk. During our conversation I noticed that Marilyn, who was wearing a dress, was in the early stages of pulling her panties down. Almost immediately, I asked what she was doing. She stopped, smiled and said, "Henry asked me to pull my panties down."

I looked directly at Henry, who had his head down. He was embarrassed and I was angry. I had not been prepared for this kind of situation but intuitively knew it wasn't good. I thought about scolding him before I erupted, "You get out of here right now and don't you ever come back." Moments later I told Mama what had happened and while she was proud of me, she made it a point to claim that this was what worldly kids do, and why we shouldn't associate with them.

An Unusual, Repressed Environment

I also fondly recall an event that occurred when I was eleven after attending two JW Thursday-night meetings. We seldom arrived home before 11:00 PM. With four kids in the family, it could be a challenge for Mama to get us into bed before midnight and we had school the next day. So on our drive home from the Kingdom Hall one night, Mama said she would give a quarter to the first one to get into bed, a dime for the second and a nickel for third. The last kid would get nothing.

Being the oldest, I decided not to play this game. But when we drove into the driveway, my three siblings were totally naked. Jumping out of the car, they raced to see who could get into bed first. Marilyn and my brother Tim were so close that Mama gave each of them a quarter; one of those crazy events that Marilyn and I reminisced as adults.

On a somber note, Marilyn and I were raised in a "sex-negative environment." We were regularly bombarded with guilt based on a strict interpretation of sexuality in the Old Testament. Mama must have constantly thought, "Have I taught my kids enough about how important sexual fidelity is to God?"

So we were thoroughly indoctrinated in how to harness the power of the sex drive in order to please God. We were often warned about sexual no-no's in The Watchtower and at the Kingdom Hall—everything from masturbation, oral sex and the role of women in the conceptual process. Sexual pleasure was never discussed.

Sex before marriage was an onerous crime and a show-stopper in God's eyes. If a person should do the unthinkable, he or she was expected to report it to an elder. A judicial meeting would be scheduled and presided over by men who didn't trust psychologists. During the hearing, details were shared—depth of penetration, how many times it was done, where it was done, whether oral sex was involved, etc. Then the elders would caucus to figure out how repentant the person was, reach agreement on what the sin was, and decide on the proper punishment for the crime.

While we were growing up, Marilyn and I didn't have a clue that we were sexually repressed. We never talked one-on-one about this subject, or any serious topic that I can remember. Nor did we have any memorable moments of "big brother - little sister" conversations. That would come later in life, when we were adults, not as children. My role as the big brother focused on protection, and I did my fair share of teasing.

A Change of Lifestyle

In the summer of 1958, I traveled with Mama to an eight-day convention of JWs in New York City. Marilyn stayed at home with Papa. During the convention attendees were told over and over that Armageddon was near and the end of the world was imminent.

However, we also were told that there were still many people in isolated parts of the U.S. that had not heard the "good news." We were encouraged to move "where the need was great." Mama talked at length with a JW official there and I could see what was incubating in her mind.

When we arrived back at our Los Angeles home, Papa and

Mama conferred alone for several days. Finally, we had a family meeting where Marilyn and I were asked if we wanted to "serve Jehovah" in a different part of the U.S., in the Midwest where snow fell in the wintertime.

Marilyn loved the idea, thinking it would be a wonderful adventure. That look of pure joy on her face, as fanciful as it was, is a look that I will never forget, a sweet memory of Marilyn's innocence. In the end, it was Mama's decision, and her decision would dramatically change our lives.

Part Two

In November 1958, my family moved to Columbus, Nebraska. Like all the homes we lived in while I was growing up, there was only one bathroom for our family of six. And Marilyn would take forever to do her business, so it could be a challenge if you really needed to go.

One day I pounded on the door, pleading for her to finish so I wouldn't pee in my pants. Finally, she opened the door and walked out. I rushed in and opened the toilet lid. After several seconds of boyish deliberation, I decided that I would call her the "Little Logger." That nickname stuck with her until the day she died.

I left home in 1962 to go to Bethel, the world headquarters for the Watchtower Society in Brooklyn, New York. Still a teenager, Marilyn was convinced that Armageddon was near and a new world was just around the corner, but she was by no means a gung-ho JW.

In fact, she was not happy with her day-to-day life. She realized that Nebraska was not the big adventure she once thought it would be. Isolated in a small, rural community, she had no friends and was not encouraged to read anything but JW literature. Bored with school and life in general, she felt like a ward in Mama's make-believe world, unable to figure out who she really was.

Shortly after Marilyn graduated from high school in 1966, she tried to find part-time work in Columbus. But with only a basic, minimal education, there were few jobs available to her except for cleaning homes and offices. She found cleaning jobs at several places, but after a few days on each job she would be terminated.

Marilyn lived at home for almost three years and could not find work. Because she could not help out financially, tension began to mount between Marilyn and our parents. Marilyn also resented the special treatment given to Susan, our mentally handicapped sister. Marilyn and Susan bickered constantly. Marilyn grew desperate and decided she needed a change of scenery.

A Surprise Phone Call

It was 1969 and I'd been an ex-JW for four years when Marilyn called me on the phone. She wanted to move to Grand Rapids, Michigan, where my wife Helen and I were living. Could she live with us for two weeks? She wanted to find a job and a place to live. I talked it over with Helen and we told her "yes". We felt this would be an opportunity to help Marilyn and to get to know her better as an adult.

However, after two days into her visit, Helen was not happy. Marilyn was doing nothing to help Helen with chores around the house. Just like Mama, Marilyn preferred to be waited on, not ever being trained to do otherwise. But to Marilyn's credit, she wasn't offended when Helen told her she needed to take more initiative.

Marilyn did find a job working for a small Chinese restaurant located at the north end of Grand Rapids, about fifteen miles from our house. My brother Tim and Helen's sister Esther, who were newlyweds, helped Marilyn find an apartment within walking distance of her job. Marilyn started attending meetings at Tim and Esther's Kingdom Hall and began dating a JW man her age. For a while, all seemed to be going well for her.

But suddenly, she informed me that she wanted to go back to Nebraska. After only four months away from home, she said that she wasn't happy, spent more money than she made, and she didn't like her job.

"The Man of Her Dreams"

Six months later she called to tell me that she had met "the man of her dreams" in Nebraska. They were going to get married and she wanted Helen, me, and our two children, Keith and Kim, to attend the wedding. Her fiancé was Jerome Roper and his extended family were well-to-do JWs in central Nebraska. Everyone liked the Roper family. She didn't know what Jerome would do for work, but his parents would help him find a job and help pay the rent for their first house.

I felt that the key ingredients for a responsible husband appeared to be missing. However, if Marilyn loved Jerome and he made her happy, why shouldn't I be happy for her?

Three months after they were married, Marilyn and Jerome came to visit us. Jerome, a carefree sort of guy, seemed disconnected from Marilyn. He hinted about staying in Grand Rapids, if I could get him a job at the company where I worked.

When I first met his brothers and dad at Marilyn's wedding and reception, I had a feeling they had good work ethics, but that's not how I sized up Jerome.

A day into their visit, Jerome asked if some evening he and I could go to a strip bar. He assumed that since I wasn't a JW, I liked "worldly things." While I wanted to correct him, I played along, pretending that I could arrange it. Then he let me in on a little secret: he liked hard-core pornography. When I asked if Marilyn knew about it, he said yes. She didn't like it, but they were "working on it."

The next day, I told Marilyn about my conversation with Jerome. She was pleased that I had confided in her, but disappointed that I hadn't shamed him for his poor behavior. Stunned, I told Marilyn that I thought she had a problem on her hands. Nothing I could say or do to this guy would change him. He was a self-centered little boy, disguised in a man's body. Leopards don't change their spots...

Marilyn was even-tempered, making it fairly easy to share bad news with her. She grabbed my hand and told me how grateful she was for our little talk. She confided that Jerome could also be a control freak and had been abusive. Not in a physical way, but he could go off on verbal rants that made our handicapped sister's use of the F-word seem like child's play.

They stayed with us for another day and then went back to Nebraska. In less than a week, Marilyn annulled their marriage.

(While I am getting ahead of myself, I would like to report an email I received from Jerome in 2014. He had read a portion of Marilyn's story in a blog I had written. He was one of the more fortunate, as Jerome was able to escape Watchtower's undue influence and go on to lead a happy, productive life.)

This Time "the Real Deal"

Three years later in 1972, Marilyn reported to me that she had met the second "man of her dreams," but this time the guy "was the real deal." While she was on a trip to Georgia, she met "Mr. Wonderful," believing him to be an exemplary JW, albeit a new one. Ruggedly handsome, he doted on her and she loved it.

"Does he have any baggage?" I asked.

"Oh, he had a big drug problem while growing up and he hates his dad. But then he found *the truth*. People tell me that he's a changed man. He's a workaholic, whether working for a living or working for Jehovah."

Helen and I did not attend the wedding. But Marilyn and Carter, her new husband, visited us shortly after their wedding. Carter Wilcox bore no resemblance to Marilyn's first husband, intellectually or emotionally. It appeared that he was totally devoted to her and that they were truly in love.

Carter was not a big talker, but what he said made sense. He had some interesting ideas about how he could make money selling and servicing computers, and he seemed to be a business-savvy guy.

On the other hand, I thought he would be difficult to like, especially from a guy's point-of-view. He came off as a bit of a con artist and couldn't connect with Helen. For me that was not a good sign. I also sensed that Carter was uncomfortable about me being an ex-JW. And I was someone that he would not be able to control.

Marilyn and Carter bought a home in Columbus, Nebraska. To the best of my knowledge, they were a model JW couple, doing all the things that make Witnesses unique. Carter successfully started and operated a growing computer business. They did well financially and started a family, a son and daughter.

But Marilyn's children weren't born until after I was disfellowshipped in 1977, an event that triggered Carter's decision to shun me. It was also a decision that Marilyn honored, so I was never a presence in their children's lives.

Ironically, it wasn't until 1981 that "shunning" became the official policy for all Jehovah's Witnesses. That's when my parents and brother started shunning me.

Reconciliation and a Reunion

Marilyn and I did not communicate with each other for fourteen years. However, that came to an abrupt halt when I received a surprise telephone call from her in the spring of 1991. It was a surreal experience hearing her voice again.

She couldn't apologize enough; she had waited way too long before daring to call me. She had heard that my 30-year high school reunion would be held in Columbus that summer and wondered if Helen and I were going. She hoped we would be there and wanted to renew our relationship. I hadn't planned to go to the reunion, but decided immediately that I would open the door to this opportunity.

Marilyn invited us to dinner at her house. She and Carter were separated, but her kids would be there. My parents and our sister Susan, all of whom I hadn't seen in over ten years, would also be there. I didn't say anything, but this news was a huge red flag. This made no sense unless Marilyn was in some kind of trouble. If JWs shared a meal with me, they could be disfellowshipped and shunned.

Yes, she and Carter were separated, but that's all I knew. At that point I had no idea how low our brother Tim had stooped to uphold an inhumane JW policy.

To tell this part of the story, I must go back in time and share events before Marilyn's call:

The JW policy Carter cherished most was that men are allotted special privileges over women. A man is the head of his house and king of his home, regardless of his intellectual or emotional status. This gives him certain special rights. If he wants to verbally abuse his wife, he can do so with impunity, as long as he does it with his wife's best interests in mind.

Early in their marriage, Carter had been verbally abusive to Marilyn, ratcheting it up ever so slowly as the years passed. Verbal abuse was not a new experience for Marilyn. Ironically, Mama had a talent for using it and performed her verbal magic on Papa for as long as I can remember. Papa tolerated it, so why couldn't Marilyn? After all, Carter generously provided for her physical needs and was a "good JW."

However, three years before Marilyn called me, Carter physically abused her for the first time and that scared her. While he did not abuse her regularly, he was not averse to making threats. She learned later that these bouts occurred shortly after he took swigs from a bottle of whiskey he had hidden in the basement.

Early in their marriage, Carter was verbally abusive about Marilyn's poor housekeeping, being late, and getting on his nerves "for no good reason." After the children were born, his tirades increased. Marilyn handled constructive criticism well and I'm convinced that if Carter had picked his battles and not attacked her self-esteem, it could have been a win-win for both of them.

The bottom line is no woman (or anyone else) should be subjected to the way Marilyn was treated. What made Carter's abuse even worse was that around other JWs he acted like a perfect gentleman. He would go into his rants when the two of them were alone, although a few times he had gone on short rants when their kids were around.

In an effort to get him to stop, she said that she planned to go to the elders at her Hall and report Carter's abuse.

Marilyn Decides to Ask for Help

That turned out to be a dicey strategy because our brother

Tim was serving as one of those elders and Carter was an elder as well. Carter knew what Marilyn was planning to do. He decided to help his cause by asking to meet with Tim privately.

He described to Tim how delusional Marilyn could be, particularly since the birth of their children. Carter explained how his efforts to improve her parenting and housekeeping skills were met with her pat complaint, "You're abusing me."

Carter wanted to "stack the deck" in his favor by effectively painting Marilyn as a "wacky" woman. He convinced Tim that "Marilyn was the problem" because she was refusing to cooperate and fighting Carter's leadership as head of the family.

Carter Believed He Should Be Able to Pull Marilyn's Strings

When Marilyn met with the elders—Carter had been excused—she told them everything, especially her concern about Carter's daily verbal abuse. She also mentioned that Carter had physically hurt her several times. She believed that it was possible that after drinking too much, he might kill her. The meeting went on for an hour. Tim spoke first and suggested that she might be "imagining" some of her complaints.

"What if he kills me? What happens then?" she asked.

Tim's response was typical for a JW elder. "Marilyn, that won't happen. But if it should, you will always have the hope of a resurrection if you've been a loyal and faithful wife."

"Okay, but I think a trial separation would help both of us."

Tim again responded, "Marilyn, Carter is the head of your house. If he decides that's an appropriate response, so be it. But it will be his decision."

Exasperated by the meeting, Marilyn went home fearing for her life. She knew Carter would soon learn about the meeting and the elders' recommendation.

The next two weeks were a living hell for her. Carter took his abuse to a new level, threatening bodily harm if she went to the elders again. Marilyn's self-esteem slid to a new low. She tried praying, hoping Jehovah would intervene.

She talked several times with Mama, but Marilyn had been doing that for years. And Mama's standard pat response was: "Let's just wait on Jehovah. He knows all and will take care of it in His own due time."

After two weeks, Marilyn knew that she could no longer live with Carter in her house. For her it was like living with a serial killer, knowing that it was only a matter of time before he exploded.

She had to do something—and she had to do it now!

Part Three

Desperate, Marilyn called a local Columbus, Nebraska attorney and asked if she could meet with him. It took over an hour to explain what her life had been like, particularly for the last five years. A second meeting was scheduled, and then a third.

Marilyn finally summoned the courage to do what she knew she had to do. She didn't want a divorce, knowing that adultery and death were the only two ways to end a marriage per JW rules. At the same time she did not want to live with Carter or allow him to reside in her house.

When the papers were served and Carter was forced to move out of the house, Marilyn heard from the elders at her Hall immediately. They wanted to meet right away because what she had done did not match with the Bible and their rules.

At the meeting, the elders advised her that she would have to take him back if she expected to "stay in good standing with Jehovah." They suggested that she and Carter should then take their problems to Jehovah God and He would help them mend their marriage.

Marilyn again asked, "So what if I take him back and he really does kill me this time; then what?"

The elder in charge of the meeting responded with, "You will be resurrected in the New World." For him, it was that simple. But Marilyn had the courage to stand up to him and make it clear that if that was her only option, it did not sit well with her.

The elder, who happened to be our brother Tim, explained that if Marilyn did not take Carter back, the committee would not be able to actually disfellowship her. Nevertheless, the elders would be obligated to shun her whenever she attended meetings and in other social settings. It would be their way of helping her see God's great wisdom in this matter and that their actions might ultimately help save her marriage and restore her standing with God.

A "Loving Arrangement"

According to the Watchtower, "shunning is a loving act used to help bring rule-breakers back into God's favor."

I believe shunning is the sinister trademark of any person or group that is guilty of undue influence.

I had never heard of a situation where "shunning" was an option without a person actually being disfellowshipped. I am certain that someone from Watchtower headquarters advised Tim in this matter, but no one would talk with me about it. So I assumed this decision came from Bethel's legal department, concerned about how poorly it would play out in the court of "worldly" public opinion.

The fact was that neither Marilyn nor Carter had committed adultery. Marilyn, because she feared for her life, did not want to live with Carter. After the elders made it clear that under their rules she could not kick him out of their house, Marilyn decided to ignore their advice and used the court system to remove him.

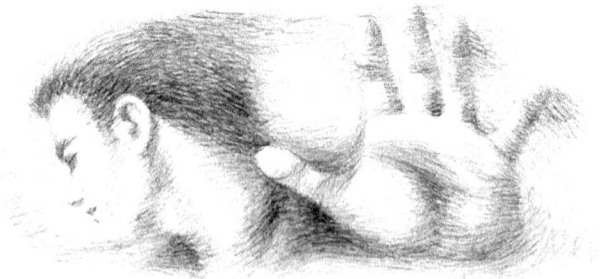

Per JWs, "Shunning" is a Loving Act to Help Bring Rule-Breakers Back into God's Favor

The events of the next six months tested Marilyn's faith as a JW. When she attended meetings with her kids, the elders and their families would not speak to her and treated her as if she was invisible. On the other hand, when Carter attended meetings he was treated as though *he* was the one who had been abused.

My Parents Take a Stand

My parents were the one exception. They knew what Carter was like and decided to take a stand. They wouldn't be disfellowshipped for talking to Marilyn, but their actions were construed as having a less than satisfactory relationship with Jehovah. So Papa was removed as an elder and told that he could no longer give public talks.

My parents consulted with other respected JW members and asked for advice. They were told that there was a "loophole"—if they were willing to use it. If they moved to another congregation (there was one in Central City, forty miles away), the members at that Kingdom Hall would not shun Marilyn. Papa would still not be eligible to serve as an elder, but he could worship Jehovah as he saw fit.

Plans were made and within three months, Marilyn's house (in spite of Carter's protests) and my parents' home were sold. After they purchased new homes in Central City, it appeared that the "dark side" of Carter and the unjust JW policy enforced by the elders had just been parts of a bad dream.

Marilyn shared those events with me after the fact, and only in dribbles and drabs. Just when I thought, "My God, can this get any worse?" I would learn of new developments.

In retrospect, I am not sure who appalls me more: Carter; The Governing Body for the Watchtower Society and the policy makers for JWs; or my brother Tim? In the end, they all harmed not just my sister, but it would be Marilyn's son and daughter who would bear the brunt of the emotional damage from that shunning experience.

Mama knows the damage done to Marilyn's children is irreparable, but somehow she is able to live with that fact. Why?

Because she believes that in the New World Marilyn's kids will grow to perfection, their childhood trauma will be forgotten, and they will live happily forever on a paradise earth. She accepts that they were inconvenienced in this lifetime, but feels that it will be well worth the wait.

Our Trip to Nebraska

When I met Marilyn at her Columbus home in August of 1991, I knew that she and Carter were separated. But I had no idea of the ordeal that she had gone through or would yet encounter.

Shortly after Helen and I checked into our Columbus motel, I called for directions to Marilyn's house. While driving from the motel to her home, we passed the Kingdom Hall on Highway 81, the same Hall I had attended from 1959 to 1962. Many unpleasant memories flooded my mind, when suddenly I noticed Carter mowing the lawn. He did not see us, but I wondered what he might do if he knew we would be meeting and spending time with his children in a few minutes.

Marilyn knew we were coming and stood on her lawn, jumping up and down as we parked the car in front of her house. Tears were streaming down her face. We had been separated for over fourteen years. The joy I felt during that initial hug cannot be put into words and I cry every time I try. Neither of us wanted to let go. Finally she said, "Please come in. I want you to meet my kids." That, too, was an emotional experience and difficult to describe.

First, I picked up Edith, a plump, smiling little girl, as pleased to see me as I was to see her. Whatever Marilyn had told Edith about me had to be very good. And Edith was the spitting image of Marilyn at that age, just bigger boned. But she had a severe stutter and it took forever for her to say anything.

I knew that no one is born a stutterer. Something had happened, possibly something Carter could have done.

Marilyn then dragged me into Willy's room. A very handsome boy with curly hair, he looked like I imagined Papa would have looked as a child. Willy knew we were there, but he was more interested in finishing the painting project he was working on.

I suspect that we could have walked out of the room and he would not have noticed, but I decided to sit down next to him and asked if I could help. He looked up and seemed pleased that I wanted to help him. Suddenly he decided we were friends and did not want me to leave.

After playing with Willy for several minutes, I excused myself because I knew Marilyn wanted to show me her house. As she directed the tour, she told me that she had called my parents and our sister Susan. They were on their way, looking forward to seeing me after all these years, and would join us for dinner. I had been excited about connecting with Marilyn, but I was uncertain of how I would feel about meeting with my parents. They hadn't spoken to me for the past ten years.

When Mama and Papa walked into the house, they were very excited to see Helen and me. Mama bear hugged me, saying how happy she was to see us. I looked older, she said, but as handsome as ever. Papa seemed just as pleased to see us and kept asking how we were doing.

No tears were shed and I was ambivalent about the experience. After all, Mama told me ten years before that unless I decided to love Jehovah as she did, she would never talk to me again. Here she was acting like nothing had ever happened. I had no idea why she could now greet or share a meal with me.

I remember eating that dinner—a meal Marilyn had worked long and hard to prepare. But in her emotional state, the meal was not up to her normal standards. The chicken and vegetables were over-cooked and tasteless. The potato was hard as a rock, and the salad lifeless. It seemed so strange that Marilyn and my parents belonged to a religious group that made it a "crime" to eat food with people like me and Helen. And yet, I'm thinking, "Why on this one occasion, when they had decided to break the rule, couldn't they have dished up a better meal than this?"

Our conversation during dinner amounted to general chit-chat and table talk that works with strangers, but not for people who were at one time immediate family. I was unnerved by it, although Marilyn and my parents appeared oblivious to this disconnect. I wanted to have one-on-one heart-to-heart chats with both Marilyn and Mama; those conversations happened later that evening and the next day.

But how totally different those two conversations turned out to be...

Part Four

When I talked alone with Marilyn, she acknowledged her duplicity. She had lost touch with basic human decency due to a poorly-thought-out JW policy. She regretted that she had shunned me for so many years. She wanted me back in her life. We had a long, candid conversation, shedding many tears. But not once did she say a word about how poorly she had been treated by Tim and Carter, nor why she could now talk and eat with me.

I talked one-on-one with Mama the next day. We had our conversation at her house, but Mama's tone and subsequent reaction was totally different from the one with Marilyn. Mama could not see the world through any other lens than her own. She was cold and hard, with no remorse. She wanted to be in total control of the conversation and refused to answer several of my questions, offering no explanation for why she could now talk with me.

Several hours into my conversation with Mama, I heard the phone ring in the next room. Papa picked it up. Later I learned that Carter had called, yelling at Papa for having the audacity to allow his kids to share a meal with me in the house he owned. He ranted on and on about me being the essence of evil. He thought Papa facilitated the crime and Papa would hear from the elders about this.

Marilyn had told me about Carter's obsessive hatred for me the day before. Carter blamed the failure of their marriage on me. It made no sense, but Carter needed a scapegoat. Papa listened to him talk on the phone without any response for fifteen minutes. At the end of Carter's tirade, Papa thanked him for calling and hung up.

Papa interrupted my conversation with Mama to give us a full account of the call. When I asked for an explanation, Mama said that Carter could be crazy at times and it was best to let him rant. It was obvious that Mama was getting more upset with each accusation. Finally, she suggested that I leave. She was tired and they planned to go to the circuit assembly the next day. That's the last time I talked with Mama before she called me five months later to see how I was doing.

When Helen and I arrived back in Grand Rapids, Marilyn started calling me on the phone two to three times a week. On Saturdays, we would talk for as long as two hours at a time. In bits and pieces, I learned about her story.

Carter reported to the elders that his kids shared a meal with me in his home. He wanted justice and he wanted Marilyn and my parents punished. The elders didn't talk to Marilyn about the incident, but they talked with my parents. What was said, Mama would never tell me.

Carter started writing letters to Marilyn, asking for reconciliation, saying she needed help, couldn't she see the damage done to the kids, and more. He cut the power lines to the house once. He disconnected the phone and cable connection several times. Clever enough to make it look like worn wires, he methodically ratcheted his diabolical plan to get her to come back to him.

Shortly after Carter was asked by the court to leave the house, Marilyn enrolled full-time at a local two-year college in Columbus. She wanted to earn an associate degree so that she could become a paralegal. She also started reading books about emotional intelligence, psychology and natural science; all books that good JWs would never read.

She wanted my opinion on the new things she was learning. For the first time in her life, she began to think on her own. What a joy it was to be a party to her new world of knowledge. It was like seeing the desert come back to life and blossom after a long summer rain. My little sister was coming out of her cocoon.

It's my opinion that at some point in Marilyn's life, probably shortly after she was shunned at her Hall, that she started to question for the first time the policies and beliefs of Jehovah's Witnesses, particularly those related to women. Up until then, she believed that God had franchised Jehovah's Witnesses with *the truth*. She started looking, albeit very slowly at first, for some new truth. Looking was the key. She should have started as a child, but it was better late than never.

The JW experience for women, especially for girls who grow up in it, is nonstop dogma about God using men to lead, teach, make judicial decisions and govern because men have been gifted with these inalienable rights. A woman's role in the church is subservience to a man's leadership. Little wonder that many JW women have this constant, nagging feeling of inadequacy.

After Attending College, the Ghost of Inadequacy Would No Longer Haunt Marilyn

In 1993, Marilyn turned in her resignation notice as a Jehovah's Witness and she divorced Carter. While Carter haunted her by renting a home across the street from where she lived in Central City, she made the best of a bad situation. It did not stop her from continuing her education and she did her best to raise her two children in an unnerving, dysfunctional setting. And I must give credit to my parents, as they tried to help Marilyn as much as they could.

But Marilyn, like many ex-JWs, was haunted by ghosts, making it difficult to break totally free from the clutches of a high-control religion. When she graduated with honors at the community college in Columbus, that learning experience helped

93

minimize the damage from the *Ghost of Misinformation*. The toxic residue from the many years of learning so many things that ain't so can be debilitating.

The most damaging ghost for Marilyn was not a ghost she could see nor did she fully understand. The deadly ghost was the *Ghost of Dependency* and her fatal attraction to highly controlling men.

When People Spend Many Years in a High-Control Religion, They Will be Haunted by Insidious Ghosts, the Toxic Residue from the Experience, when They Try to Leave.

The next part of Marilyn's story is very difficult for me to put on paper. So I will try to be short and to the point when I tell you that she married again. One of the things that she liked about her new husband was that he promised to take care of her. He would be the head of the family, a very loving head. While he was not a JW, he claimed to be very religious and God-fearing.

She attended a local Lutheran church with him and they tried to make a Brady-Bunch family—Marilyn's two kids and his four boys—work. All went well for six months before Marilyn's new husband allowed his violent nature, his intense need to control, surface.

Marilyn called me a day after it happened. His anger had not been directed at her, but at one of his boys. It scared her and she wanted my advice. Maybe he was having a bad day. He had more temper tantrums but they were always directed at his kids. Then Marilyn was the target for one of his angry tirades. He agreed to go with her to a counselor. But it would be two steps forward, three steps back. Finally, she decided to file for divorce and move to Grand Island.

While she was alone in her apartment on April 11, 1998, her estranged husband broke into the house. No one knows what was said or how he worked himself in, but before he left, he had knifed my sister to death. The coroner reported ten to fifteen stab wounds on her body.

When my parents didn't hear from Marilyn the next day, they called the police. Three days later, Mama called to tell me the bad news. When I asked about the funeral plans, she said coldly, "Marilyn's been cremated. She's dead and there's nothing we can do about it." Marilyn's brutal murder had little impact on Mama as far as I could see.

Unlike Mama, Marilyn's death strongly affected my life. For a while, I struggled with unanswerable questions: How do you make sense of a senseless crime? How could anyone hate so much that they are willing to kill, to murder someone? I quickly realized that finding answers would not bring her back. I needed to find a healthy way to bring closure to such a devastating loss.

Soon afterward, I attempted to do something totally out of character, something I had no business doing—I wrote a book, then another. If Marilyn's story could help other people, then I would learn how to write. Perhaps her story, told along with mine and Helen's, would inspire just one person to alter her or his life course, to do something that she or he would not have otherwise done. That is my hope. I could not be happier that I did it. That is what big brothers do.

Marilyn Kelly at age 25

An Afterthought

It has been seventeen years since Marilyn's tragic death and I have had much time to reflect. I have forgiven myself for not recognizing the dangerous man who her third husband turned out to be. And maybe, if Marilyn had stayed a JW, she would be alive today. Mama tells people that I facilitated her departure.

96

I have forgiven Mama for raising Marilyn in a man-made make-believe world. Mama thought it was what God wanted her to do, but it was based on lies told to her over and over by the Watchtower Society. It is the policy makers of that out-of-touch Society of old men that I am unable to forgive.

The leaders and policy makers of the Watchtower Society are heartless charlatans, a men's-only high-control religious group that champions a sexually repressive environment. It clings to out-of-date policies for which it is not currently held accountable. It makes bold claims that they are the only group directed by God.

It is a very sick group of religious leaders that sets up its followers, in particular the children of its followers, for some kind of fall: whether it's divorce, sexual abuse, sexual dysfunction, pedophilia, emotional abuse, adultery, a bad marriage, suicide, isolation, premature death, schizophrenic behavior, or depression.

Would Marilyn's life have had a different ending had she not been raised as a JW? No one will know for sure. Perhaps her attraction to abusive men was in her DNA. But I don't think so.

What I do know is that Marilyn would have wanted people, especially girls and women, to learn from her mistakes, from Mama's mistakes. Looking for real scientific truths should be a life-long journey for everyone.

If a person is looking for the ultimate truth about a God, the possibility of life after death and those kinds of things, now that is another thing. In the pursuit of that kind of truth, Marilyn would tell you, "No one knows for sure, and please don't let anyone, especially a high-control religious group, tell you otherwise."

The End

(At least until my fourth book)

Love you, Marilyn, and you too, Mariuca.

Marilyn Merges with Mariuca and Carl's Story

It had been my original intention to tell Mariuca's and Marilyn's stories along with five other remarkable women. But there was a change in plans. Now, I will write about these other five ladies and their extraordinary against-the-odds escape from Watchtower's undue influence, in what will be my fourth book, *Looking for the Truth—It's Not at Mama's Club*. "So why the change of plans?" you ask.

During a long Skype conversation between me, Mariuca and Marilyn's son, who escaped from the Club five years ago, I decided it was best to *forever connect* Marilyn and Mariuca by telling their stories in one book.

You should also know that the relationship between Mariuca, Carl and me has blossomed into something I could not have imagined. Writing their against-the-odds story was like a birthing experience for both me and my wife.

Letting go of toxic relationships is part of the healing process for those of us who were once unduly influenced and are now shunned by our immediate families. And, it has provided us with a unique opportunity. We can replace former family members with people we really like and love; people who have been there, done that. And so it is. Mariuca and Carl are now part of our extended family.

One of the gifts that Carl gave me after writing their story and reading my first two books was a print-art picture and description of me, which I have included in this book. You be the judge of evaluation of the author of this book.

Another life highlight for my wife and me was hosting Mariuca and Carl at our Tucson home in October 2014 and sharing the natural beauty of our adopted state of Arizona and one of the Seven Wonders of the World, the Grand Canyon.

The final picture, before sharing the clear and present danger of *undue influence,* is one taken in Tucson, Arizona of Helen, Mariuca, Carl and me in March 2015. We had just celebrated Mariuca's 50th birthday, a first for her, in San Diego, California, a few days before. We had driven back to Tucson, wanting to share Mariuca and Carl with our good friends, Bob and Claire Rogers, who took the picture.

A Compassionate Man of Respect (Linocut* 9x12 2014) by Carl Wilson**

This is a portrait of Richard E. Kelly sitting in his home as represented by the Arizona desert, while enjoying a fine bottle of wine. Richard's sister, Marilyn, is pictured as a mysterious figure casting a giant shadow which intersects with his. That shadow emphasizes the inextricable link between the two. She has forever influenced every action and motivation in his life since her untimely death in 1998.

A Bible engulfed by flames is seen between the two. Richard has exposed the Bible, as interpreted by Jehovah's Witnesses, as being utterly ridiculous and harmful to humankind. The Watchtower's misrepresentation of the Bible was the catalyst for the flames that destroyed Marilyn and left Richard in grief.

How ironic that the most compassionate and sensitive man in the world looks like he may leave a horse's head in your bed at any given moment. I thought about the image of Michael Corleone sitting in a room in the dark. I see Richard with that type of power, carrying the burden of the work he has undertaken. Work liberating the minds of those imprisoned by phony spirituality and religion. Work that can only be performed with the utmost compassion for fellow humans so completely lost.

* A linocut is a printmaking technique and a variant of woodcut in which a sheet of linoleum is used for the relief surface.

** You can check out other works of the artist, Carl Wilson, at www.carlwilsonart.com

A picture taken of Richard, Helen, Mariuca and Carl in October 2014 at the Grand Canyon

March 14, 2015, in Tucson, Arizona, seven days after we celebrated Mariuca's 50th birthday in San Diego.

Mariuca and Marilyn

Undue Influence

While sharing Mariuca and Marilyn's personal stories in this book, I often refer to Watchtower's psychological control over the thoughts and emotions of members as *undue influence*. For many, these words, this phenomenon will be something new.

By adding this section, my goal is to help you understand about the growing menace of *undue influence* and how quickly it can happen in the manipulative hands of terrorist groups, cults masquerading as benevolent religions, violent gangs, human traffickers and extreme political cults, be they left or right wing.

These groups violate basic human rights and siphon away resources that could be used to resolve other major problems in today's world. The reason these sinister groups get away with it has nothing to do with ideology; rather, they have adopted the devious art of *undue influence* and we are all too often oblivious.

What Is Undue Influence?

Undue influence happens when a person is persuaded to act against his or her better interests, usually for the benefit of a group or person intent on exploiting that person; and it is a legal term that has been understood and used in courtrooms for over 500 years to protect victims of *undue influence*.

Whenever someone or a group takes advantage of a position

of power over another, *undue influence* is at work. It is *influence* by which someone is induced to act without proper attention to the consequences.

Undue influence is synonymous with *thought-reform* and *brainwashing;* and one can add *mind control, coercion, unethical influence, mind manipulation, uninformed consent, extreme social influence, indoctrination, propaganda, mental abuse, emotional abuse, emotional blackmail, menticide, thought control, re-education, coercive persuasion, intense social-psychological control,* and *exploitative persuasion* to the list. All of these terms are valid, and their very existence demonstrates how widespread the phenomenon is.

By focusing on *undue influence* I hope to increase the resistance of millions of people, preventing *undue influence* from derailing critical thinking and overwhelming even the most intelligent of people, reducing them to unthinking compliance.

How and Why Do People Allow Themselves to be Unduly Influenced?

When *undue influence* is imposed on unsuspecting recruits by most high-demand groups and cults, it typically begins with flattering "love bombing" and idealistic promises. The recruit may be promised eternal life, a world without injustice or offered élite status in a better society that the group will bring to fruition.

The hook for terrorist groups, like ISIS and Al Qaeda, is the promise that years of injustice toward Muslims will be undone, and a restoration of the glory days of the Caliphate, when Islam governed half of the known world.

Once recruits have bought into the promises and hyperbole, they are introduced to a systematic method of control: one small step at a time.

This methodical system of control—*undue influence*—disrupts the person's authentic personality and constructs a new identity in the image of the group's leader or leaders. In the process, the ability to think rationally and act independently is compromised, even for people considered "highly rational" prior to being *unduly influenced.*

Undue influence occurs when the overall effect of the methods to control behavior, information, thoughts and emotions promotes dependency and obedience to a cause, leader or group. Members of high-demand groups and cults being *unduly influenced* can live in their own homes, have 9-to-5 jobs, be married with children, and still not think for themselves or be able to act independently.

What Kinds of Groups and People Use Undue Influence?

The dangerous effects of *undue influence* are easy to spot in groups like Islamic State (Daeth or ISIS), which boldly claims to be a legitimate religious movement. Its use of *undue influence* to radicalize young people, in pursuit of its agenda, has led to some shocking examples of human depravity. One does not need to be a psychology major to realize that mass executions and public beheadings do not follow the "free will" or normal behavior of otherwise bright, educated young men unless *undue influence* had been brought to bear by their autocratic leaders.

Other groups that *unduly influence* their members to suppress personal and critical thinking skills are pseudo-religious groups like Jehovah's Witnesses; Scientology (which masquerades as a benevolent religion); human traffickers; some multi-level marketers; terrorist groups like ISIS; violent extremist gangs, including the Crips, the Bloods, and the Hell's Angels; internet gurus; political sects (extreme left or right wing); paramilitary groups; pimps; Identity Christians; survivalists; human potential hucksters; Neo-Nazis; Transcendental Meditation cults; Skinheads; Aryan Nations; the LaRouche Organization; Hare Krishnas; White and/or Black Supremacist groups; some trade associations; Moonies; totalitarian governments, such as North Korea; and abusive spouses and parents.

These high-demand groups, cults and abusive people are not only guilty of *undue influence*: they egregiously violate the fundamental human rights of their members, former members and those people and groups that oppose them.

While each of these groups is different and distinct, their common ground is a similar methodology—*undue influence*—used to undermine the critical thinking skills of members and replace them with the leader's or group's objectives and a polarized *us-against-them* and *black-or-white* mentality.

How Great of a Threat is Undue Influence to a Free Society?

It is a significant threat to fundamental human rights and a free society when *undue influence* is used to behead and murder innocent people, crash passenger planes into buildings, break up families, deceive followers to shun family members, order parents to beat their children under "biblical commands," persuade people to break the law, cheat people out of their inheritance or property, turn adolescents into slaves and prostitutes, threaten parishioners with shunning if they report child molestation or domestic violence to the police, or coerce parents into allowing their children to die, because it is supposedly "God's will" or accords with the master plan of a high-demand group or leader.

One of the most alarming consequences of *undue influence*, rather than religious ideology, is the radicalization of young intelligent men and women, who come from good families and become recruits for aberrant Islamic groups like ISIS, Al Qaeda or the Mahdi Army. The propaganda war being played out on social networking sites is growing across Europe and becoming increasingly devious and seditious in its capacity to alienate potential recruits from family and friends.

The *undue influence* process can occur very quickly, anywhere from one day to two weeks. Currently, the UK police are taking down a thousand websites a week. The potential for accelerated growth in the industry of radicalization is very real, extremely dangerous and toxic to society as a whole. As radicalization grows, so must the countermeasures of methodology to inoculate and pacify this threat.

Unfortunately, governments have tended to take advice from a handful of academics who dismiss the social influence processes used to radicalize young Muslims into Wahhabi ideology. (We have to differentiate the Wahhabi tendency, just as we would say

'Branch Davidians at Waco' rather than 'Christians at Waco')

Additional costs to society from groups that unduly influence its members

Many of these high-control groups and cults have tax-exempt or even charitable status, which means citizens pay the taxes for any properties they own and the services required to maintain those properties.

While these tax exempt groups receive billions of dollars from members, they *do not* recycle that money into the local and/or global community to improve society, instead funneling it to the leaders, while members often live in poverty. In other words, there is a deplorable absence of socially beneficial works.

To meet the demands placed upon them, many members of cult-like groups are subsidized by the social welfare system, costing society even more money, because these groups rarely provide any health care for members.

How Can We Stop This Rapidly Expanding Menace to a Free Society?

The big picture

Universities and high schools need to educate students to identify *undue influence* and inoculate them from its harmful potential. Funds and grants should be allocated for research and treatment for victims of *undue influence*.

Reform in the public education system is urgently needed to teach people how to think for themselves and make independent decisions, rather than simply instilling obedience. Students should be taught *intelligent disobedience* and encouraged to question established beliefs and behaviors.

Whistle blowers should be supported, rather than attacked, and devil's advocacy encouraged to overcome our tendency to groupthink.

Therapists must be better trained to help victims assimilate back into society with online training courses and internet resources available to all. Governments need to end tax breaks for groups that use *undue influence* to manipulate their members.

Documentary films, like Gregorio Smith's *Truth Be Told or* Alex Gibney's *Going Clear*, which address the culture of *undue influence,* need to be watched, and more films about *undue influence* need to be produced.

Individuals, families and lawyers need to work together to create legal precedents and frame generic lawsuits to improve redress for *undue influence* victims.

Universities and qualified research teams should be encouraged and assisted to accurately report the costs to society of *undue influence*.

At a personal level

The general public can be protected from *undue influence* by studying material that offers rational and evidence-based approaches to life, ethics and history. People need to learn to be open-minded and prepared to question what they are told by others and what they read. This includes a willingness to disagree agreeably and to consider new evidence carefully, even when it goes against their convictions and biases.

People need to make their own decisions about right and wrong, good and evil, harm versus help, and the greater good versus the benefit of the few. Everything should be judged on overall benefit, not only to ourselves, but to those around us. If a politician or self-styled "prophet" tells us that he or she alone has the absolute truth, those claims should be treated with the utmost skepticism.

We should never let a day go by without resisting and exposing those who try to influence us by shaming, threatening or shunning. We should take every opportunity to educate our families and friends to the dangers of *undue influence* so we can protect them from harm.

Special needs

Some people subjected to *undue influence* were recruited, while others were born into unethical, high-demand groups and cults. These are very different experiences and require different solutions. It is especially difficult for those born into such groups to escape the conditioning, because they will have no awareness that they have been conditioned.

There is another huge problem for those people who want to leave a cult, but have been subjected to many years of *undue influence*. While they may physically leave, the cult's confrontational mentality of "us-against-them", "we're right, you're wrong", "black-and-white thinking", a highly judgmental view of people who don't think and believe as they do and an insatiable need to tell others what is right and wrong does not leave them. This is compounded by the guilt and phobias they have unknowingly acquired while being *unduly influenced*.

If this is not bad enough, many people are trapped in relationships and totalist cults and are unable to escape. Because of the fear of shunning, black mail, being unable to take care of themselves outside the group or threat of bodily harm, they remain.

The need for therapy

Because people are often unable to rid themselves of the cult mentality, along with the trauma of severe shunning, there is a huge need for well-trained therapists who understand the process of *undue influence*. In fact, many ex-cult members will never fully recover unless they spend time with a competent therapist.

If you visit a therapist, you should be careful to ask these questions at your first session, which are adapted from *Take Back Your Life* by Gillie Jenkinson at www.hopevalleycounselling. com. "And remember," says Gillie, "you do not have to continue with the first therapist you see. Don't be afraid to interview the therapist to make sure he or she will be the one most likely to meet your needs."

But there are potential risks to therapy, especially for survivors of therapy cults such as Scientology. Therapies that seek to relive the trauma of membership are flawed; hypnotherapy often does not achieve the desired result and people can become dependent upon therapy.

For many people complete recovery may come from informal therapy with other ex-members who have fully recovered. The most significant therapy can occur after a lively discussion about the principles of the group.

Available resources

Information is available to help people understand how undue influence works and to help them expel the toxic residue from it. This information can help victims transform their lives from the group's identity to their authentic identity.

Recommended books to read are Jon Atack's *Opening Minds: The secret world of undue influence, thought reform, brainwashing...* Janja Lalich's and Madeline Tobias's *Take Back Your Life: Recovering from Cults and Abusive Relationships* and Steven Hassan's *Combating Cult Mind Control.*

Robert Cialdini's *Influence* is used in universities around the world, as is Aranson and Pratkanis's *Age of Propaganda.* Other books are available, but this is a good place to start if you want to understand how *undue influence* works.

Professor Khapta Akhmedova recommends Jon Atack's *Let's sell these people A Piece of Blue Sky* for an understanding of the dynamics of cultic involvement. Paralleling is the best way to understand your own involvement, without feeling challenged, so this is useful for non-Scientologists. *Blue Sky* has proved useful because, with its vast array of techniques, Scientology is the microcosm of almost all possible cult practices.

Best Practices & Resources

There are pockets of success about groups and people who are successfully educating the public about *undue influence*. They are creating a greater awareness of the prevalence and danger of *undue influence* and helping victims to recover.

1. A good example is Sweden's EXIT Fryshuset, an organi-

zation that helps members escape from violent extremist groups that *unduly influence* their members, and that helps victims to re-integrate into society. EXIT was launched in 1998 and has since operated successfully with rehabilitation and preventive work. They also coach relatives of active Neo-Nazis, consult and educate professionals who come in contact with these individuals (in schools, social services, police force, etc). Their website is at: http://exit.fryshuset.se/english/and https://www.counterextremism.org/resources/details/id/63/exit-fryshuset

2. Another best practice can be found at: http://www.ontmaskermanipulatie.nl/ This Dutch website allows visitors to respond anonymously to a 26-question questionnaire. If a person scores 50% or higher, they are being *unduly influenced*.

3. If one lives in The Netherlands and suspects that either he or she, or a friend is being *unduly influenced*, they can call a hotline funded by the Dutch government. The caller will talk with someone who has been trained in the use of *undue influence* by high-control groups and cults. The callers will also be helped if they want to escape. The call center is open 7 days a week from 10:00 am to 5:00 pm. One can find out about this service at: http://www.sektesignaal.nl/

4. In Switzerland, the government funds an educational help group that responds to requests for information about cult-like groups at http://www.infosekta.ch/

5. Another gem that is worthy of a visit is ICSA at www.icsahome.com. Founded in 1979, the International Cultic Studies Association is a global network of people concerned about psychological manipulation and abuse in cultic or high-demand groups, alternative movements, and other environments. ICSA supports civil liberties, and is not affiliated with any religious or commercial organizations. ICSA is unique in how it brings together former group members, families, and how it helps professionals and researchers.

6. The largest data base of material relating to cults and *undue influence* is the Fight Against Coercive Tactics Network, FACTNet www.factnet.org

7. Alexandra Stein, Ph.D. is an educator and writer, specializing in totalist cults and dangerous relationships. Get to know

Alex at www.alexandrastein.com

8. Gillie Jenkinson is a therapist's therapist helping people recover from cults and abusive relationships. Connect with her at www.hopevalleycounselling.com

9. Steve Hassan is a writer and tireless crusader helping people get out destructive relationships and cults. Check him out at freedomofmind.com

10. Alan W. Scheflin has championed *undue influence* as a university professor for many years. His article, "Supporting Human Rights by Testifying Against Human Wrongs" (6 International Journal of Cultic Studies 2015-Pages 69-82) is a masterpiece.

11. Masoud Banisadr makes a convincing case for *undue influence* and why it, and not ideology, drives terrorism in aberrant Islamic groups. His book "Destructive and Terrorist Cults: A New Kind of Slavery" is a reveling read, although he prefers to use the words *mind manipulation* instead of *undue influence*.

The Need for Research Projects

The public and media definitely need many more completed research projects to validate the harm and cost of undue influence by unethical high-control groups. One such project was performed by Dr. Flavil Yeakley, albeit a long 30 years ago:

In 1985, the Boston Church of Christ asked Flavil Yeakley, a personality test expert, to make a study of its members. Critics insisted that the group caused unhealthy transformation of personality in its members. The Boston Church of Christ was accused of being a cult that was brainwashing its members.

Over 900 members filled in extensive questionnaires. Yeakley also administered the Meyer-Briggs' Type Indicator to 30 members each of six groups generally regarded as "manipulative sects" (Yeakley's expression), which included Scientology, The Way, the Unification Church (or Moonies), the Hare Krishna Society, Maranatha and the Children of God, and to 30 members each in five mainstream churches: Catholic, Baptist, Methodist, Lutheran and Presbyterian. The same personality test was filled out three times by most of the subjects, as if it were five years earlier; from their present perspective; and how they anticipated they would answer five years into the future.

In Yeakleys' word, 'Changes in psychological type do not indicate normal healthy growth. Such changes indicate some pressure in the environment that causes people to deny their true type and try to become like someone else. There were no significant deviations in personality type over time among members of the five mainstream churches, but *all* of the 'manipulative sects' showed significant movement, *including* the Boston Church of Christ, in direct opposition to its leader's belief that his group was not a cult.

Yeakley found there was a convergence towards a particular personality type within each manipulative sect, but that the type varied from group to group. In other words, the 'manipulative sects' were changing the personalities of their members each towards its own specific type. The effect has come to be known as 'cloning' and is a substantial proof that thought reform/undue influence occurs in some groups.

Are You Being Unduly Influenced?

Amazingly, many, many people are being *unduly influenced* and most have no idea that this is the case. Millions of people spend most of their lives without being aware of the *undue influence* that was brought to bear upon them on a daily basis. Here are ten questions to ask to see if you are being *unduly influenced*:

Does your group insist on blindly following a set of dogmatic ideals that cannot be challenged?

Does your group threaten members with shunning, if they deviate from the group's ideology?

Does your group treat its belief system as *the truth* and all other belief systems as false and the work of the devil?

Do you belong to a closed, stigmatized group that schools its members in *black-and-white thinking*, framing *soci-*

ety as conspiratorial and everyone outside the group as enemies?

Does your group decide on what is the appropriate dress code and hairstyle for members?

Does your group require you to proselytize and canvass for new members?

Does your group encourage spying and tattling on other members to find incriminating information?

Are failures and false predictions coming from the group blamed on human error, rather than upon the group's leaders or its ideology?

Do your group leaders promote feelings of guilt and unworthiness, and undermine your sense of self-worth?

Does your group instill fear and phobias about the world beyond the group, departure from the group, the fate of former believers, losing your faith or not achieving the group's *manifest* destiny: be it everlasting life, an ideal political state with no injustices, Utopia or untold riches?

A questionnaire

Another set of questions, 26 of them, is put forward by two well-respected Dutch therapists, and can be accessed online at: http://www.ontmaskermanipulatie.nl/

Where Do We Go from Here?

Much more work needs to be done, as most people just aren't aware of the real danger of *undue influence* in today's world. If you would like to help draw attention to this fast-growing menace and take actions as outlined in this chapter, please email me at mariucaandmarilyn@gmail.com or visit me at Open Minds Foundation (openmindsfoundation.org).

A Word from the Artist Who Designed the Book Cover

By Carl Wilson

The background of the cover uses slightly overlapping, faded, repeat images of Marilyn and Mariuca. This feature represents their lives as cult members, unfortunate victims of a twisted social order desirous of mass producing clone soldiers. These semi-transparent images also represent Mariuca and Marilyn's inability to be fully realized women, no fault of their own.

Those same images appear in stark presentation bearing their names. This proudly proclaims each woman with the demand they be accepted as they are. The font I used for the cover is a throwback to classic paperback novels of the seventies and eighties. I chose this font and a retro approach because I thought it was completely appropriate for the, at times, «true crime» reporter style that you write in. I find it bone chilling that you tell Marilyn's story this way because sadly, it is a true crime story.

I tried to bring continuity to the design by emphasizing the Mama's Club brand and retaining the color palette used in the previous books.

Thanks for the opportunity. I have served as an art director and graphic designer in the past. It's not an easy job because there can be so many people of differing taste to satisfy, but yours is a labor of love. That makes it a labor of love for me also.

Carl Wilson reflecting on the graphics for the book's cover

Acknowledgements

I want to thank four very special neighbors and good friends, Catherine Stevens, Ken Hake, Gilda Dick and Stacey Haines. All of these great people love to read and have carefully critiqued the first draft of this book. Their suggested changes, comments and editing skills have helped make this book so much better.

I would also like to thank my "undue influence" mentors and friends, Steven Hassan, Jon Atack and Masoud Banisadr. They have played a significant role in helping me understand how pervasive undue influence is, violating a person's thoughts and emotions. What's so interesting about their scholarly advice is that they too were involved in a harmful cult. Steven spent several years as a Moonie, Jon a Scientologist and Masoud with a terrorist and aberrant-Islamic group.

Alex Stein, an outstanding mental health consultant, and Gillie Jenkinson, a therapist extraordinaire, have inspired me with their knowledge, expertise and passion. I only wish my sister Marilyn had known about people like Alex and Gillie, when she was leaving Watchtower's culture of undue influence. Fortunately Mariuca and Carl received the help they needed to recover their authentic identities.

John Hoyle is one of those friends and confidantes that most people can only dream about. John's good advice and compassion have been a big help to me in writing this book. He is also a tireless webmaster who has helped me and many other people use the internet to report to the public about our personal stories of dealing with Watchtower's undue influence.

I am also very grateful to Helen, my wife of 51 years, for her love and patience. Without that, it would have been very difficult, if not impossible, for me to pursue my love of writing, and getting to know the people I choose to write about.

I also want to thank Mike White, of Ghost River Images, for helping me publish this book, as well as my other two Mama's-Club books. He is a man among men when it comes to writing books and getting them published.

The artwork for the book cover is a gift from creative genius Carl Wilson. And his depiction and picture of me in the high desert of southern Arizona graces my office and now this book. Please check his artwork at www.carlwilsonart.com.

www.ingramcontent.com/pod-product-compliance
Lightning Source LLC
Chambersburg PA
CBHW061745020426
42331CB00006B/1357